Holocaust

Holocaust

THE NAZIS' WARTIME JEWISH ATROCITIES

STEPHEN WYNN

Pen & Sword
MILITARY

AN IMPRINT OF PEN & SWORD BOOKS LTD.
YORKSHIRE - PHILADELPHIA

First published in Great Britain in 2020 by
PEN AND SWORD MILITARY
An imprint of
Pen & Sword Books Ltd
Yorkshire - Philadelphia

Typeset in Times New Roman 11.5/14 by
Aura Technology and Software Services, India
Printed and bound in the UK by TJ International

Pen & Sword Books Ltd incorporates the Imprints of Pen & Sword Books
Archaeology, Atlas, Aviation, Battleground, Discovery, Family History, History,
Maritime, Military, Naval, Politics, Railways, Select, Transport, True Crime, Fiction,
Frontline Books, Leo Cooper, Praetorian Press, Seaforth Publishing, Wharncliffe and
White Owl.

For a complete list of Pen & Sword titles please contact

PEN & SWORD BOOKS LIMITED
47 Church Street, Barnsley, South Yorkshire, S70 2AS, England
E-mail: enquiries@pen-and-sword.co.uk
Website: www.pen-and-sword.co.uk

or

PEN AND SWORD BOOKS
1950 Lawrence Rd, Havertown, PA 19083, USA
E-mail: uspen-and-sword@casematepublishers.com
Website: www.penandswordbooks.com

Contents

About the Author

Stephen is a happily retired police officer having served with Essex Police as a constable for thirty years between 1983 and 2013. He is married to Tanya who is also his best friend.

Both his sons, Luke and Ross, were members of the armed forces, collectively serving five tours in Afghanistan between 2008 and 2013. Both were injured on their first tour. This led to Stephen's first book: *Two Sons in a Warzone – Afghanistan: The True Story of a Fathers Conflict* (2010).

Both of his grandfathers served in and survived the First World War, one with the Royal Irish Rifles, the other in the Mercantile Navy. His father was a member of the Royal Army Ordinance Corp during the Second World War.

Stephen collaborated with Ken Porter on *German PoW Camp 266 – Langdon Hills* which spent six weeks as the number one best-selling book in Waterstones, Basildon, between March and April 2013, and since then Steve and Ken collaborated on a further four books in the Towns & Cities in the Great War series by Pen and Sword. Stephen has also written other titles in the same series, and in 2017 *The Surrender of Singapore – Three Years of Hell 1942-45* was published. This was followed in 2018 by *Against All Odds: Walter Tull the Black Lieutenant*.

Stephen has also co-written three crime thrillers, published between 2010 and 2012, about a fictional detective named Terry Danvers.

When he is not writing, Tanya and he enjoy the simplicity of walking their three German Shepherd dogs early each morning, at a time when most sensible people are still fast asleep in their beds.

Introduction

My late father's step-sister's husband is Jewish, and when I knew that I was going to be writing this book, I decided that I would ask him about his family, as I had a distant memory from when I was a child that he had lost some of his relatives during the holocaust.

He and my father used to work together on the buses, in fact when my father died in 1970 it was he who broke the news of his death to me when I returned home from school, at around four o'clock on one Thursday afternoon.

Years later I bumped into him by chance in a local shop. The conversation turned to writing and I told him that I was going to be writing this book. It was then that I asked him whether he would talk to me about his family and the holocaust. Without a moment's hesitation, he replied, 'no I can't' – politely, but firmly. 'It's too painful and I just can't talk about it, and to be honest, it is not something that I *want* to talk about.' I understood his reluctance.

The Holocaust saw Jews and other groups marginalised, persecuted, and murdered *en masse* by the forces of Nazi Germany. I would suggest it has its roots as far back as 30 January 1933, when Hitler was made Chancellor of Germany. On 1 April 1933, Hitler declared a national boycott of Jewish businesses. This was quickly followed on 7 April with the Law for the Restoration of the Professional Civil Service, which meant that all non-Aryans, which of course included Jews, were no longer allowed to practice law, medicine, education or be a member of the civil service.

From 1933, the Nazis began building a series of concentration camps across Germany for political opponents and those they deemed 'undesirable', which basically meant anybody they didn't like. Throughout the Second World War, the Nazis established a staggering 42,000 concentration camps, detention sites and ghettos, most of which were for Jewish people.

The Enabling Act, passed on 23 March 1933, gave Hitler powers to enact laws without the involvement of the Reichstag. He was given absolute power to take action on any issue, however he saw fit, with no limitations.

On 6 May 1934, members of the German Student Union forced their way into the library of Magnus Hirschfield's Institute of Sex Research. Hirschfield was a physician and sexologist. All the books held at his library were removed by the students. On 10 May 1934, more than 25,000 books were burned in the square at the State Opera in Berlin by students.

The Night of the Long Knives took place over three days between 30 June and 2 July 1934. It consisted of a number of coordinated attacks on Hitler's more powerful enemies. Estimates of the numbers killed range from 85 to 250.

The anti-Semitic Nuremberg Laws were enacted on 15 September 1935. They forbade marriage and extramarital intercourse between Jews and Germans. Only those of German or related blood could be classed as Reich citizens, the remainder were now classed as state subjects with no citizen's rights.

With the 1936 Olympics taking place in Berlin, the last thing Nazi Germany wanted was any bad press, so until the event was over, nobody was prosecuted under the Nuremberg Laws.

Those Jewish people who understood that things were only going to get worse for them tried their best to leave the country, but to do so wasn't easy. Those wishing to leave were required by law to hand over 90 per cent of their wealth to the Nazis as a tax on leaving the country. By 1938 it had become even more difficult, as by then it was nigh on impossible for them to find a country that was willing to accept them.

This book examines the planning of what the Nazis referred to as the Final Solution, along with the Warsaw ghetto and the uprising which led to a violent armed revolt in the spring of 1943. The book also explores the different Nazi concentration camps, and the methods and means by which they went about disposing of millions of innocent Jewish people. The final part of the book looks at when the Allies first knew of these atrocities, and why for so long they did nothing about it.

Chapter 1

The Odessa Massacre

On 22 October 1941 a radio-controlled mine exploded at the headquarters of the Romanian 10th Infantry Division. The device had been set by soldiers of the Red Army before they had surrendered the city of Odessa to the Romanians. The entire building collapsed, killing sixty-seven people, mostly military personnel, sixteen being Romanian officers. One of the dead was General Ioan Glogojeanu, the Romanian military commander of Odessa. The incident was blamed on the Jews and the Communists.

The Odessa Massacre, 1941.

The next day a combination of Russian troops and German Einsatzgruppen arrived in Odessa and killed an estimated 5-10,000 hostages, mostly Jews. In Marazlievskaya Street, people broke into the homes of Jewish residents, killing anybody they found, either by shooting or hanging. Those not murdered were led away and driven to Lustdorf Road where there were a number of warehouses. All those who had been rounded up were either shot dead or burned alive. After the war mass graves were discovered there containing some 22,000 bodies.

The same day an order was issued by the Romanian Army for all Jews to report to the village of Dalnik. Any who didn't and were found would be shot on the spot. About 5,000 Jews turned up at Dalnik as ordered. Most were brought to a large freshly dug anti-tank pit and shot. Others were herded into four large barracks and machine-gunned by soldiers of the Romanian 10th Machine Gun Battalion under the command of Lieutenant Colonel Nicolae Deleanu. Afterwards, the barracks were set on fire. The following day more Jews were placed in another two barracks, machine-gunned, and finished off with grenades.

Some were sent back to their homes, but en route were told to attend either military headquarters or police stations to be registered. After they were registered they were detained for a time, during which their homes were broken into by the authorities and personal property was stolen.

By November 1941 the Romanian authorities had established that there were nearly 60,000 Jews in Odessa. They were ordered to wear a yellow Star of David emblem. On 7 November 1941 the Romanian authorities issued an order:

All men of Jewish origin, aged between 18 and 50 years, are obliged within 48 hours from the date of publication of this order, to report to the city prison [in Bolshefontanskaya Road], *having with them the essentials for existence. Their families are obliged to deliver food for them in prison. Those who do not obey this order and are found after the expiration of the indicated 48 hour time period will be shot on the spot.*

All residents of the city of Odessa and its suburbs are required to notify the relevant police units of every Jew of the above category who had not complied with this order. Coverers, as well as persons who know about this and do not report, are punishable by death.

[Signed] *Lieutenant Colonel M. Niculescu, head of Military Police for Odessa.*

The cruel treatment of the Jews didn't stop there. Soon the deportation of the Jews of Odessa to concentration camps began. The camps had been set up in the countryside by the Romanians, the main camp being near the village of Bogdanovka.

By 20 December 1941 the number of Jews being held at the Bogdanovka concentration camp had reached 55,000. Between that date and 15 January 1942, every last one of them had been shot either by German SS Einsatzgruppe troops, Romanian soldiers or Ukrainian police.

Still the killing didn't stop. In January 1942, an estimated 42,000 Jews were evicted from their homes in Odessa and sent to a ghetto that had just been set up near a town named Slobodka. There were not enough buildings to house them all, so many had to live outdoors and perished to hypothermia. The 19,582 survivors were sent to Bereza, in the Odessa region, between 12 January and 20 February. Many of them didn't make it, either dying from starvation, the weather, or by being shot by the guards who were escorting them, who were mainly German.

By this time there were only about 1,300 Jews left in Odessa. Some 700 had gone into hiding, the others had somehow managed to survive the horrendous conditions of the ghettos where they had been sent to live.

After the war, in 1946, the Bucharest People's Tribunal, which had been jointly set up by the Allied Control Council and the new Romanian government, brought charges against Marshal Ioan Antonescu, Gheorghi Alexianu (the governor of Transnistria who was also the commander of the Odessa garrison), and General Nicolae Macici (who was responsible for the repressions against

Odessa's civilian population in the autumn of 1941). All three were sentenced to death for their crimes. General Macici had his death sentence commuted to life imprisonment by King Michael of Romania. Antonescu and Alexianu were executed by firing squad on 1 July 1946.

Chapter 2

The Wannsee Conference

The Wannsee Conference, named after the suburb of Berlin in which it was held, was a meeting of senior government officials of Nazi Germany and leaders of the SS. It was called by SS Obergruppenführer Reinhard Heydrich, who had been tasked with putting in place the Final Solution to the Jewish Question. Before Nazi Germany could begin the process of systematically murdering millions of Jewish men, women and children, the cooperation all of the different government departments, along with the Waffen SS, the Gestapo, and the army, had to be assured.

It was actually Hermann Göring who started the ball rolling by writing to Heydrich on 29 November 1941 with instructions to submit a plan for the Final Solution. Heydrich would have found no ambiguities in what he was being instructed to do.

One of the first things that Heydrich had to come up with was a definition of what constituted an individual being classified as a Jew. Included in this equation would be individuals such as Anne Frank's father, Otto, who was a German citizen and had served with the German Army during the First World War, and the lieutenant who had recommended Adolf Hitler for his Iron Cross during the same war. But as far as Heydrich was concerned, emotions or an individual's previous history were irrelevant. Heydrich understood that there would be some at the meeting who wouldn't be in agreement with his proposal, and others, even if they were, would find his methods distasteful. In an effort to alleviate this aspect of his proposal, he emphasized that once the deportations had taken place, the responsibilities of the exterminations would purely be a matter for the SS.

A copy of Heydrich's proposal for the Final Solution, along with minutes of the meeting which had taken place at Wannsee in Berlin on 20 January 1942, survived the war. Whether it was meant to or not is uncertain, but survive it did. In March 1947 it was discovered amongst files recovered from the German Foreign Office in Berlin. They were found by one Robert Kempner. Kempner, in 1928, when chief legal adviser to the Prussian Ministry of the Interior, had tried to prosecute Adolf Hitler for the offence of High Treason and to have the Nazi Party classified as an illegal organisation. Unfortunately he wasn't successful in either case. He was dismissed from the Prussian Ministry of the Interior and his German citizenship was revoked by Wilhelm Frick, a prominent member of the Nazi Party who served as the Reich Minister of the Interior in Hitler's Cabinet for ten years until 1943. Frick was tried and found guilty at the Nuremberg trials on 1 October 1946 and hanged fifteen days later.

After his isolation from German society, Kempner emigrated to Italy in 1935 before ending up in America in 1939. After the end of the war he returned to Germany as assistant United States chief counsel at the International Military Tribunal that was held in Nuremberg. In a twist of ironic fate, Kempner ended up prosecuting both Frick and Hermann Göring.

The minutes of the Wannsee Conference showed that the Nazis had estimated Russian and Ukrainian Jewish populations somewhere in the region of eight million.

The meeting had originally been intended to take place on 9 December 1941 at a different location in Berlin, with invitations sent out on 29 November. Each invitation included a copy of the letter Heydrich had been sent by Göring, instructing him to make preparations for the Final Solution.

Between the date of the invitations being sent out and the date of the intended meeting on 9 December, the war unexpectedly changed considerably. On 5 December, Russian forces took the war to Germany when they began a counter-offensive outside Moscow, just as the Nazi leadership had believed they were about to deliver the Soviet Union a *coup de grâce*. Two days later, Japanese forces attacked Pearl Harbor in Hawaii, which resulted in the United

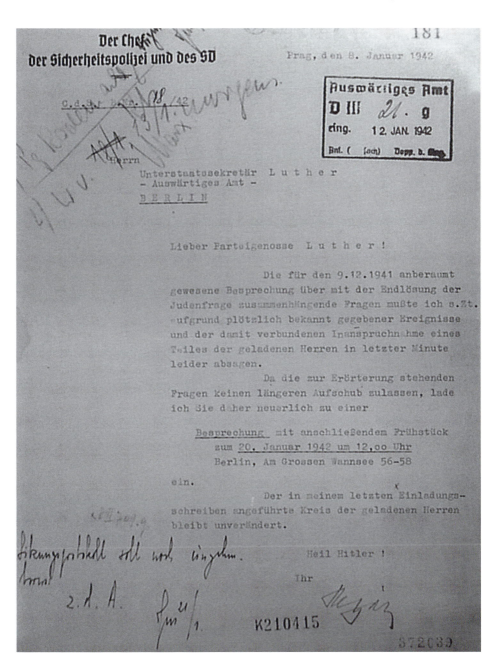

181

Der Chef der Sicherheitspolizei und des SD

Prag, den 8. Januar 1942

G.d.St.b.Nr. 18 /42

```
Auswärtiges Amt
D III  21 . g
eing.  12. JAN. 1942
Bnf. (    [ach]    Dopp. d. Eing.
```

Herrn

Unterstaatssekretär L u t h e r
– Auswärtiges Amt –
B E R L I N

Lieber Parteigenosse L u t h e r !

Die für den 9.12.1941 anberaumt
gewesene Besprechung über mit der Endlösung der
Judenfrage zusammenhängende Fragen mußte ich s.Zt.
aufgrund plötzlich bekannt gegebener Ereignisse
und der damit verbundenen Inanspruchnahme eines
Teiles der geladenen Herren in letzter Minute
leider absagen.

Da die zur Erörterung stehenden
Fragen keinen längeren Aufschub zulassen, lade
ich Sie daher neuerlich zu einer

Besprechung mit anschließendem Frühstück
zum 20. Januar 1942 um 12,oo Uhr
Berlin, Am Grossen Wannsee 56–58

ein.

Der in meinem letzten Einladungs-
schreiben angeführte Kreis der geladenen Herren
bleibt unverändert.

Heil Hitler !

Ihr

K210415

372039

The letter from Reinhard Heydrich to Martin Luthor, inviting him to the Wannsee Conference.

States declaring war on Japan on 8 December. This in turn led to Germany declaring war on the United States on 11 December 1941. These events appear to have changed Hitler's intentions with the Jews, because despite Göring's letter to Heydrich, dated 29 November 1941, a Reich Chancellery meeting took place on 12 December 1941, which would have included all top members of the Nazi Party. No minutes of the meeting survive. However, in an entry of the diary of Joseph Goebbels, Hitler's Minister of Propaganda, he recorded the following:

> *Regarding the Jewish question, the Führer has decided to make a clean sweep. He prophesised to the Jews that if they yet again brought about a world war, they would experience their own annihilation. That was not just a phrase. The world war is here, and the annihilation of the Jews must be the necessary consequence.*

Up until this moment, Hitler had viewed the Jews as some kind of bargaining chip, but with America now in the war on the side of the Allies, they no longer had any value to him. His long term plans to exterminate the entire Jewish population once the war in Europe was over had now changed and became more immediate.

There are a couple of questions which need answering. First: why did Germany feel the need to declare war on the United States just four days after the Japanese had attacked Pearl Harbour? She had no need to do so, but took the decision anyway, turning a European conflict into a global one.

Second: how could Hitler have only announced his intentions regarding the 'Jewish problem' at the Reich Chancellery meeting which took place on the afternoon of 12 December 1941, when Göring had sent his letter to Heydrich instructing him to prepare a plan for the Final Solution on 29 November 1941? Maybe with Göring's letter to Heydrich there was no urgency to the implementation of the Final Solution and it was only meant to be put in place once the war was over. If so, then all of that changed on 12 December 1941.

Once the commotion of December 1941 had died down, Heydrich sent out new invitations on 8 January 1942. The villa where the conference took place was owned by the *Sicherheitsdienst*, or the Security Police of the SS.

There were fifteen people present at the Wannsee Conference, who represented several different sections of the German government.

Reinhard Heydrich, of the SS, presided over the meeting. He was to be assassinated in Prague on 4 June 1942.

Otto Hofmann worked for the SS department of Race and Settlement. After the war Hoffmann was tried at Nuremberg, found guilty and sentenced to twenty-five years imprisonment, beginning his sentence at Landsberg Prison in Bavaria. On 7 April 1954, having served just six years of his sentence, he was released and pardoned. He died in 1982.

Heinrich Müller was another SS man in charge of the Gestapo. He was last seen in the *Führerbunker* in Berlin on 1 May 1945. Although it is believed that Müller was more than likely killed during the fighting of those final days before Russian forces captured Berlin, his body was never recovered and he remains the last most senior Nazi figure who has not been accounted for.

Karl Eberhard Schöngarth was an Oberführer in the SS. He was sent to Krakow in Poland as a senior commander of the *Sicherheitspolizei*, or Security Police, as well as the SD, which was the intelligence agency of the SS and the Nazi Party. Between July and September 1941 he was responsible for the deaths of some 10,000 Jews. He was also believed to have been involved in the murder of 263 Dutch civilians in a reprisal killing for the attempted murder of Hans Albin Rauter, an SS Obergruppenführer, on 8 March 1945. After the war he was captured and tried by a British Military Court at Burgsteinfurt, not for the murder of 10,000 Jews or 263 Dutch civilians, but of a downed British pilot on 21 November 1944 at Enschede, Holland. He was found guilty, sentenced to death, and hanged on 16 May 1946 at Hamelin prison by British executioner, Albert Pierrepoint.

Gerhard Klopfer, an Oberführer in the SS who worked as a permanent secretary of the Nazi Party and as an assistant to

Martin Bormann, escaped from Berlin in May 1945. He was later captured, imprisoned and charged with war crimes, but when investigated further, there was found to be insufficient evidence against him and he was released. In civilian life he practised as a lawyer. He died in 1987, the last of those who attended the Wannsee Conference.

SS Obersturmbannführer Adolf Eichmann was the minute-taker at the Wannsee Conference. Eichmann and his department became responsible for the deportation of hundreds of thousands of Jews from across Europe to concentration camps for extermination. Eichmann brought to the meeting a list of the number of Jews who lived in each country. For England the number was 330,000.

Rudolf Lange had been the commander of the *Sicherheitspolizei* in Latvia and the Baltic states. He was also in charge of Einsatzkommando 2. Lange oversaw the extermination of an estimated 24,000 Jews from the Riga ghetto in November 1941, part of what has become known as the Rumbula Massacre. In May 1942 Lange gave the order for the remaining Jews in the Daugavpils ghetto to be murdered. Lange's body was never found, nor was he ever recorded as having been captured by the Russians. He was wounded during the fighting of the Battle of Poznan. The assumption is that he either died of his wounds or committed suicide when the Russians finally seized Poznan on 23 February 1945, after a dogged resistance of the city's German garrison.

George Leibbrandt wasn't a military man or a member of the SS or the Gestapo, he was a bureaucrat and a diplomat, and held positions in both the Nazi Party Foreign Policy Office and the Reich Ministry for the Occupied Eastern Territories, where he was an expert on Russian-related matters. At the end of the war Leibbrandt was detained and kept in Allied internment from May 1945 until May 1949. It wasn't until January 1950 that he was formally charged with involvement in the destruction of the Jews, but the case against him was dismissed and he was released. He died in Bonn aged 82.

Alfred Meyer was Gauleiter of North Westphalia between 1939 and 1945. At the Wannsee Conference he represented the Reich

L a n d	Zahl
A. Altreich	131.800
Ostmark	43.700
Ostgebiete	420.000
Generalgouvernement	2.284.000
Bialystok	400.000
Protektorat Böhmen und Mähren	74.200
Estland - Judenfrei -	
Lettland	3.500
Litauen	34.000
Belgien	43.000
Dünemark	5.600
Frankreich / Besetztes Gebiet	165.000
Unbesetztes Gebiet	700.000
Griechenland	69.600
Niederlande	160.800
Norwegen	1.300
B. Bulgarien	48.000
England	330.000
Finnland	2.300
Irland	4.000
Italien einschl. Sardinien	58.000
Albanien	200
Kroatien	40.000
Portugal	3.000
Rumänien einschl. Bessarabien	342.000
Schweden	8.000
Schweiz	18.000
Serbien	10.000
Slowakei	88.000
Spanien	6.000
Türkei (europ. Teil)	55.500
Ungarn	742.800
UdSSR	5.000.000
Ukraine 2.994.684	
Weißrußland aus- schl. Bialystok 446.484	
Zusammen: über	11.000.000

List used at the Wannsee Conference showing the numbers of Jews living in different countries.

Ministry of Occupied Eastern Territories. He used slave labour, mostly Jewish, on numerous building projects. With the war coming to an end and Nazi Germany to be the vanquished nation, Meyer committed suicide on 11 April 1945.

Joseph Bühler was a state secretary and deputy governor in the Nazi controlled General Government in Krakow. At the Wannsee Conference Bühler spoke of solving 'the Jewish question … as quickly as possible'. After the war Bühler was tried in Poland for crimes against humanity and hanged on 22 August 1948.

Roland Freisler was State Secretary of the Ministry of Justice and President of the People's Court. In the First World War he won the Iron Cross 1st Class, as well as being wounded and taken prisoner by the Russians. Freisler was somewhat of an enigma as he was not that well thought of within the higher echelons of the Nazi Party, in particular Adolf Hitler. There were two main reasons for this: firstly there were rumours, which he always denied, that he had collaborated with his Russian captors whilst a prisoner of war. Certainly he learnt to speak Russian, took an avid interest in Marxism, and when repatriated to Germany in 1919 had on his paperwork the word 'Commissar'. The other thing that went against him was his brother Oswald, also a lawyer, who had on more than one occasion acted as defence counsel in cases challenging the Nazis' right to rule. It is surprising in the circumstances that Freisler was invited to the conference. He didn't make it to the end of the war. On 3 February 1945 he was holding a session of the people's court when Berlin came under attack by a B-17 aircraft of the US Army Air Force. Freisler ordered everyone to make their way to a nearby air-raid shelter. But he remained behind to gather some files and was killed.

Wilhelm Stuckart was also a lawyer and a state secretary in the Interior Ministry during the Second World War. In 1933 he joined the army and by 1944 was an SS Obergruppenführer. He attended the Wannsee Conference to deputise for his boss Wilhelm Frick, the Interior Minister. Stuckart said at the conference that he would support forced sterilization of persons who were of mixed race instead of extermination. Stuckart argued that only persons who had two Jewish grandparents should be sterilized by force, and that they should then be allowed to remain in Germany and live out their lives. Stuckart said at the meeting:

> *I have always maintained that it is extraordinarily dangerous to send German blood to the opposing side. Our adversaries will put the desirable characteristics of this blood to good use. Once the half Jews are outside Germany, their high intelligence and education level, combined with their German heredity, will render these individuals born leaders and terrible enemies.*

This would not have gone down well with all of those at the meeting. Stuckart was also concerned about the distress that would be caused to German spouses and the children of interracial couples. There would not have been too many people in the inner circle of Nazism who would have had such worries.

Stuckart was arrested by the Allies and tried in April 1949 at Nuremberg for being involved in the formulation and exacting of 'Jewish laws'. The prosecution referred to him as an 'ardent Jew hater'. Stuckart told the court that he supported the forced sterilisation of people who were of mixed race purely to prevent even more drastic measures from being implemented. His defence claimed that over time he lost his faith in Nazism and had made numerous requests to be released from his position to join the army, all of these requests being rejected personally by Hitler. He was sentenced to time already served and released. He died in 1953 near Hanover, in a car accident which some suspect was murder.

Erich Neumann joined the Nazi Party in May 1933. At the Wannsee Conference he represented the Ministries of Armaments and Ammunition, Economy, Finance, Food, Labour and Transport. Neumann requested that all Jewish workers who were working for firms involved in essential war work were not deported for 'the time being'. After the war he was arrested by the Allies in 1945, but released due to poor health in 1948. He died three years later.

Friedrich Wilhelm Kritzinger was a state secretary in the Reich Chancellery during the Second World War. He had joined the Nazi Party in 1938. Immediately after the Wannsee Conference, Kritzinger tried to quit his position in the Reich Chancellery, but his resignation was not accepted. Kritzinger was arrested after the war and appeared at the Nuremberg trials not as a defendant, but as a witness. He declared that he was ashamed and disgusted at the atrocities committed by the Nazis. He was not charged with any crimes and was released, but died in Nuremberg the next year.

Martin Luther was an under-secretary in the Reich Foreign Ministry. He had joined the Nazi Party on 1 March 1933 and went on to become an advisor to von Ribbentrop, the Foreign Minister of Nazi Germany between 1938 and 1945. It was Luther's copy of the minutes of the Wannsee Conference that were discovered in the archives of the Reich Foreign Ministry in 1947, without which the Allies would not have known that the meeting had taken place.

Luther was an interior designer, which he continued to do during the war when he could find the time. He helped von Ribbentrop's wife Annelies with the interior design of some of her homes, but he resented the job, as he wasn't paid for it and she treated him like one of her servants.

In 1943 he tried to oust and replace Ribbentrop as Foreign Minister, but failed. Von Ribbentrop, not a forgiving man, had Luther sent to Sachsenhausen concentration camp. Hitler too was incensed and ordered Luther hanged. But Luther was a friend of Himmler, who saved him from hanging and ensured that he worked in the camp's herb garden.

During his incarceration Luther tried to commit suicide on more than one occasion. He remained at the camp until he was liberated by Russian forces in April 1945. His freedom was brief, as he died soon afterwards of a heart attack.

The Wannsee Conference lasted only ninety minutes, but historically it has become an important event in the chronology for Nazi Germany's Final Solution.

The conference was opened by Heydrich who told the attendees what anti-Jewish measures had been taken since the Nazi Party came to power. He explained that in the eight years since 1933, a total of 537,000 German, Austrian, and Czechoslovakian Jews had left their

Inmates at Sachsenhausen concentration camp.

countries. The report that Heydrich had in front of him, prepared by Eichmann, showed that there were roughly eleven million Jews in the whole of Europe. Of these, about half lived in countries under German occupation. He explained that any further Jewish emigration had been prevented from taking place by Himmler, and that because of this, a new solution to the problem would have to be found. Initially this would happen in the form of 'evacuating' Jews to the east. This, he said, would only be a temporary measure and a step towards the Final Solution. Heydrich spoke for nearly an hour, after which there were thirty minutes of questions.

Eichmann, who took the minutes of the meeting, later said:

> *The gentlemen were standing together, or sitting together and were discussing the subject quite bluntly, quite differently from the language which I had to use later in the record. During the conversation they minced no words about it at all. They spoke about methods of killing, about liquidation, about extermination.*

Heydrich told Eichmann after the meeting what should and shouldn't appear in the minutes, and that they were not to be verbatim. Later, at his trial, Eichmann said, 'How shall I put it, certain plain talk and jargon expressions had to be rendered into official language by me.'

It has to be remembered that by the time of the Wannsee Conference the murder of Jews by Nazi Germany was nothing new. It started soon after German forces invaded Poland, and by the time of the conference tens of thousands of innocent Polish, Serbian, and Russian Jews had already been murdered by the Germans.

Originally there had been a plan to send Jews to the parts of the Soviet Union that had been occupied by German forces after its successful invasion. Once there, they would have been worked to death as slave labourers as part of new road building schemes. But after Germany's advance into Russia faltered in the winter of 1941, it was all change. The following are the words of Heydrich at the Wannsee Conference on the topic of relocating Jews to the east for slave labour purposes:

> *Under proper guidance, in the course of the Final Solution, the Jews are to be allocated for appropriate labour in the East. Able-bodied Jews, separated according to sex, will be taken in large work columns to these areas for work on roads, in the course of which doubtless a large portion will be eliminated by natural causes. The possible final remnant will, since it will undoubtedly consist of the most resistant portion, have to be treated accordingly, because it is the product of natural selection and would, if released, act as the seed of a new Jewish revival.*

Adolf Eichmann

At the end of the war Eichmann was arrested by American forces. After spending time in several camps, he managed to escape from a camp at Cham in Bavaria while out on a work detail. He had gone undetected while in the custody of the Americans because he had false papers which showed his name as Otto Eckmann. Realising

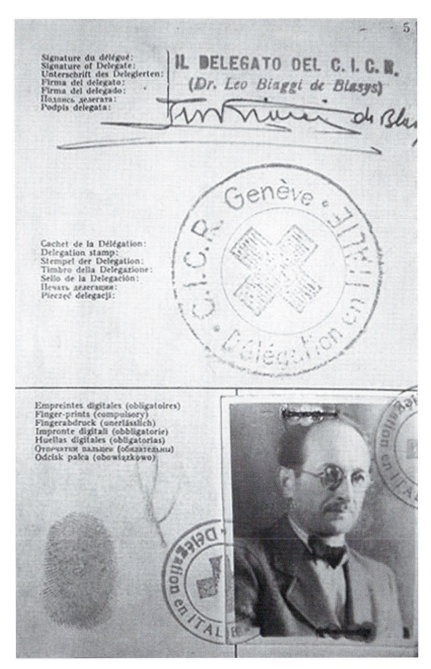

Adolf Eichmann's passport, which was used when he escaped to Argentina.

the authorities had somehow discovered his true identity, his need to escape was urgent. He didn't go far, managing to remain in Germany, but in 1950, maybe feeling the world was closing in on him, he moved to Argentina with the help of Alois Hudal, an pro-Nazi Austrian Catholic bishop.

Having acquired the relevant documents, he was then able to obtain a humanitarian passport, from the International Committee of the Red Cross, in the name of Ricardo Klement. His escape route saw him travelling across the countries of post-war Europe, with nearly all of the safe houses he stayed in being monasteries. Eichmann boarded a ship on 17 June 1950 at Genoa in Italy, and twenty-seven days later he arrived in Buenos Aires to start his new life. In 1952 he was joined by his wife and children. But it wasn't going to end

Roll call of prisoners at Buchenwald.

well, with part of his eventual downfall and capture coming, albeit unintentionally, from within his own family.

At first life was good for Eichmann and his family. He had a good job working for Mercedes-Benz and they moved in to a new home. Unfortunately for Eichmann, a number of Holocaust survivors, like Simon Wiesenthal, himself a survivor of various concentration camps, had made it their lives' work to hunt down Eichmann and the rest of his kind who had escaped justice at the end of the Second World War.

In 1956, Eichmann's son Klaus started dating a girl by the name of Sylvia Hermann, the daughter of Lothar Hermann, a half-Jewish German who had left Germany in 1938 and emigrated to Argentina. For some reason Klaus bragged about his father's Nazi past. Sylvia then told her father, who contacted authorities in West Germany, who in turn passed it on to Israeli authorities. The information was finally acted on in 1960, when on 11 May Eichmann was captured by a combination of Mossad and Shin Bet operatives outside his home in Buenos Aires, smuggled out of the country and taken to Israel.

Eichmann was tried, found guilty, and sentenced to death by hanging on 15 December 1961. After an appeal for clemency failed, he was hanged at a prison in Ramla on 1 June 1962.

Chapter 3

Operation Reinhard

Operation Reinhard was the codename for the plan to murder all Jews who lived in the General Government district of German-occupied Poland, the area established after the invasion of Poland by Germany and the Soviet Union.

One of those who had a leading role in the operation was SS Gruppenführer Odilo Globočnik. On 13 October 1941 he received an order from Himmler to begin constructing an extermination camp at Belzec. This time there was no flowering things up by calling it a 'labour camp' or a 'concentration camp': this was to be a place where people, mainly Jews, who had committed no civil or criminal offence, would be murdered on an industrial scale.

The concentration camp at Majdanek, first opened on 1 October 1941, and Auschwitz II-Birkenau, where construction work began on in October 1941, were originally designed as forced labour camps, before being turned in to death camps. They also became part of Operation Reinhard.

An interesting point to note here is that the order by Himmler

Odilo Globočnik played a leading role in Operation Reinhard.

to Globočnik to commence the building of the first extermination camp came some three months before the Wannsee Conference. It was followed by two more at Sobibor and Treblinka, with all three operational in the first half of 1942.

There is some conjecture amongst historians as to how the name of the operation was arrived at. Some believe it was named after Reinhard Heydrich, others that it was named after Fritz Reinhardt, the State Secretary of Finance who oversaw the collecting, sorting and using of confiscated belongings such as cash, jewellery, gold, clothes, shoes, bags and suitcases of the murdered victims.

Operation Reinhard finally came to an end in November 1943 when the Nazis suddenly had more important things to worry about.

Operation Reinhard's implementation was briefly delayed after Heydrich was assassinated on 4 June 1942. Heydrich's role was taken by SS Gruppenführer Heinrich Müller.

Müller first tried to use incendiary bombs for killing. This took place at Chelmno concentration camp in Poland but turned out to be ineffective, as well as setting the surrounding trees on fire. Disposal of bodies was first done by burning them on large pyres on top of large, iron grills. Any remaining bone fragments were easy to crush and were then reburied with the ashes.

Cover-up

By November 1943 the Germans were losing the war and it was time to get rid of the evidence of what they had done in the camps. This meant dismantling the camps to the degree that there was nothing left of them, killing all of those who were still alive, or transferring them to other camps back in Germany, maybe to use them as a last-minute bargaining tool.

The cover up had actually begun in May 1942 with Operation Sonderkommando-1005. The operation took two years and was undertaken in the strictest of secrecy. The work groups involved in exhuming the bodies were called *Leichenkommandos* – corpse units. These in turn were overseen by squads from the *Sicherheitsdienst*, the intelligence wing of the SS.

Burning of bodies at Auschwitz II-Birkenau (April 1945).

The bodies of some two million Jews killed in Poland during Operation Reinhard had been buried in mass graves. Himmler ordered that all such graves were dug up, the bodies exhumed and burnt.

At Sobibor many bodies had been buried in large pits immediately outside the camp. After the *Leichenkommando* had done their job, they were themselves murdered and disposed of in the same way. It was November 1942 before the work at Sobibor had been completed. The next location was Belzec, where exhumation and cremation took place around the clock until March 1943. At Treblinka the work continued until July 1943. At Auschwitz II-Birkenau and Majdanek the crematoria operated by their own prisoners.

SS-Hauptsturmführer Dieter Wisliceny gave evidence regarding the Sonderkommando-1005 section at the Nuremberg Trials. The following was his testimony:

In November 1942, in Eichmann's office in Berlin, I met Standartenführer Blobel, who was the leader of the Sonderkommando-1005, which was specially assigned to remove all traces of the Final Solution of the Jewish problem by Einsatz Groups and all other executions. Sonderkommando-1005 operated from at least the autumn of 1942 to September 1944 and was all through this period subordinated to Eichmann. The mission was constituted after it first became apparent that Germany would not be able to hold all of the territory occupied in the East, and it was considered necessary to remove all traces of the criminal executions that had been committed. While in Berlin in November 1942, Blobel gave a lecture before Eichmann's staff of specialists on the Jewish question from the occupied territories. He spoke of the special incinerators he had personally constructed for use in in the work of the Sonderkommando-1005. It was their particular assignment to open the graves and remove and cremate the bodies of persons who had been previously executed. Sonderkommando-1005 had operated in Russia, Poland and through the Baltic area. I again saw Blobel in Hungary in 1944 and he stated to Eichmann in my presence that the mission of Sonderkommando-1005 had been completed.

Despite giving evidence against his former colleagues and, helping gain convictions against both Blobel and Eichmann, Wisliceny was later handed over to Czechoslovakia where he was tried, convicted of crimes against humanity, sentenced to death, and hanged in Bratislava on 4 May 1948.

As for Blobel, whose war time atrocities included the massacres at Babi Yar and Bila Tserkva, he was convicted of crimes against humanity and hanged at Landsberg Prison on 7 June 1951.

Paul Blobel at his trial in 1948.

The massacre at Babi Yar is covered elsewhere in this book. Bila Tserkva was a town in the Ukraine, whose entire adult Jewish population was murdered by a German Einsatzgruppe and a unit of Ukrainian auxiliaries on 21 and 22 August 1941. A group of ninety children and a few women who had been left to look after them were later also shot dead in woods nearby. There were two army chaplains attached to the 6th Army of the 295th Infantry Division whose troops were responsible for the massacre: Catholic Father Ernst Tewes and the Lutheran Pastor Gerhard Wilczek. They raised no opposition to the killing of adults, but when it came to the children they wrote protest letters which were so impassioned they resulted in staff officer Lieutenant Colonel Helmuth Groscurth ordering a postponement of the planned murders of the children. But he was overruled by General von Reichenau, who ordered that the murder of the children should go ahead, which it did.

Many of the guards from these camps were sent to Northern Italy to hunt down Jews and local partisans. Globočnik was sent to the San Sabba concentration camp, where he oversaw the detention, torture and murder of political prisoners. The five-storey building that was the San Sabba concentration camp still stands to this day and is a museum in Trieste.

Chapter 4

Operation Harvest Festival

Aktion Erntefest took place during 3 and 4 November 1943 and was the single largest Nazi massacre of Jews in the war. It resulted in the murder of an estimated 43,000 Polish Jews who had been working as slave labourers at Majdanek concentration camp and its sub-camps, many of whom had previously lived in the Lublin ghetto.

Mass grave outside Majdanek concentration camp.

The mass shooting had been carried out by the *Ordnungspolizei*, the Order Police or Orpo, along with a section of Ukrainian *Sonderdienst*, who were collaborators from the Soviet Red Army.

Why did the massacre take place, and why in November 1943? Before the murders the Nazis had been surprised at how many uprisings there had been of Jewish workers working in SS slave labour projects: there had been revolts at Trawniki, Majdanek, and Poniatowa as well as at the sub-camps of Budzyn, Kraznik, Pulawy, and Lipowa. There had also been trouble at Treblinka and Sobibor, as well as Warsaw, Vil and Bialystok ghettos, when the Jewish occupants realised they were about to be murdered by the SS. With nothing to lose they revolted and fought back, and although the SS were never in any danger of being overcome, it worried them enough to come up with Aktion Erntefest.

The Nazis had decided to carry out one large-scale operation because they dared not carry the murders out one camp at a time in case word of the atrocities leaked out and there were further uprisings.

At Majdanek the labourers were informed that anti-tank trenches needed to be dug around the camp for security reasons. The plan worked and the trenches were finished without the prisoners realising they had just dug their own graves.

Although a reserve unit, the Orpo were very experienced. They had rounded up Jews to go to Treblinka and Majdanek camps, and they had carried out atrocities in the ghettos of Lublin and other areas throughout Poland. They had taken part in mass killings at the Jozefow ghetto, the Miedzyzrec ghetto, and at more than a dozen other locations the previous year.

At Majdanek, the Jewish inmates were brought out in groups to the 'anti-tank trenches' they had dug, shot one at a time, and either fell or were pushed into the pit. The man in charge of the killings was the rather strange looking Erich Muhsfeldt. By the end of the first day, 18,400 had been murdered from the main Majdanek camp. To muffle the sound of gun shots, loud music was played through loudspeakers in the camps.

In Christopher Browning's book *Ordinary Men,* he mentions that 'for a battalion of less than 500 men, the ultimate body count was at least 83,000 Jews.'

Order Police looking for hidden Jews are photographed descending into a cellar in Lublin.

Very few of the Orpo were prosecuted at the end of the war. Major Wilhelm Trapp, who commanded Battalion 101, was captured soon after the end of the war by British forces and held at the Neuengamme internment camp, which during the war had been a concentration camp. He was handed over to the Polish authorities with three other officers of the Orpo and charged with war crimes. He was found guilty and sentenced to death. His execution and that of one of the other officers was carried out on 18 December 1948.

Not until 1964 did any other members of the Orpo Reserve Police Battalion 101 face justice, and even then their sentences were light. Eleven men were arrested, some of whom had been members of the Hamburg Police at the time of the massacres. The case didn't come to trial for a further two years, then took another two years to prosecute. Three of the unit's members were sentenced to terms of imprisonment of eight years, one was given six, another five. Six other members of the unit were also arrested, tried and found guilty, but rather bizarrely not given any sentence.

No one else from the Orpo was ever prosecuted for their war-time atrocities; all lived out their lives peacefully in their native Germany.

Orpo Reserve Police Battalions 45, 101 and 103 were also involved in large-scale massacres of Jews during the Second World War. Battalion 45 was involved in the infamous Babi Yar massacre in which 33,000 Jews were murdered in woods outside the Ukrainian capital of Kiev.

In total there were seventeen Orpo Police Battalions deployed during the invasion of Poland in 1939.

Chapter 5

The Warsaw Ghetto

At the beginning of the Second World War, Nazi Germany rounded up more than three million Polish Jews and forced them to live in blocked-off ghettos. Most of Poland's larger cities had such areas, but by far the largest of them was in Warsaw, where around 400,000 Jews were restricted to an area about one and a half miles square. The following is from the Polish Foreign Ministry report of 10 December 1942:

Jewish women and children being removed from a Warsaw bunker.

The initial steps leading to the present policy of extermination of the Jews were taken already in October 1940, when the German authorities established the Warsaw ghetto. At that time all the Jewish inhabitants of the Capital were ordered to move into the Jewish quarter assigned to them, not later than 1ˢᵗ November 1940, while all the non-Jews domiciled within the new boundaries of what was to become the ghetto were ordered to move out of that quarter. The Jews were allowed to take only personal effects with them, while all their remaining property was confiscated. All Jewish shops and businesses outside the new ghetto boundaries were closed down and sealed.

The original date for these transfers was subsequently postponed to November 15ᵗʰ 1940. After that date the ghetto was completely closed and its entire area was surrounded by a brick wall, the right of entry and exit being restricted to the holders of special passes, issued by the German authorities. All those who left the ghetto without such a pass became liable to be sentenced to death, and it is known that German courts passed such sentences in a large number of cases.

Owing to inadequate food supplies for those in the ghetto, smuggling became a normality of everyday life; even the Germans were involved in the practice, as it was easy to make profits by charging high prices for basic items or foodstuffs. The food ration for the ghetto's inhabitants was a pound of bread per person per week, and that was it. Unless people could obtain food in other ways, that's all they had to eat. Prices for food in the ghetto were about ten times those outside. People quickly began suffering with exhaustion, starvation and disease. During the winter of 1941-2, 13 per cent of the inhabitants of the ghetto died. It became common to find dead bodies in the streets.

When the Warsaw ghetto was established, its population was officially stated as 433,000, and despite the high death rate, the total remained the same as more and more Jews arrived from all over German occupied Europe.

Not content with the death rate in the ghetto, the German authorities decided to help matters along by 'resettling' the Jewish population 'to the east'. Before the first of these enforced deportations began, a meeting was held with the ghetto's *Judenrat*, or Jewish Council, where it was announced that 7,000 Jews would be resettled each day.

The *Judenrat* had no power. It was simply an administrative body that Jews in the ghettos were required by the German authorities to form. It was more for the benefit of the Germans than it was for the Jews. If the Germans wanted the Jews to do something, they simply informed *Judenrat* what they wanted.

The SS codenamed the deportations *Grossaktion Warschau*. Between 23 July and 21 September 1942, 300,000 Jews from the Warsaw ghetto were 'resettled'. In reality this consisted of a train journey to an extermination camp in nearby Treblinka. Most were dead within hours of arriving at the camp.

Initially there was no resistance from the ghetto's Jewish community, as they believed in the resettlement story they had been told, or felt that at worst some of them might be sent to labour camps where they would have to undertake some kind of work for the Germans.

Deportations began on 22 July 1942. Failure to provide 6,000 people each day to meet the required quotas had severe consequences: it resulted in the execution of 100 people.

By the end of the year none of those left in the ghetto had received a single written word from any of their friends of families who had been 'resettled'. Eventually the truth of the deportations became known.

Having realised that only death awaited them, they decided their only choice was to fight. Their opportunity came on the morning of 18 January 1943, the date of Germany's second planned 'resettlement' of Warsaw's Jews to the east. While the women and children were hidden away in bunkers, Jewish resistance fighters took on the German soldiers when they entered the ghetto. The resistance fighters suffered heavy losses, which was not unexpected against a well-drilled and disciplined German force. The Germans suffered

The Warsaw ghetto showing both sides of Żelazna Street.

sufficient casualties to make them call a halt to the intended deportations after a few days and withdrew, but not before they had taken another 5,000 Jews from the ghetto.

The resistance fighters knew that they didn't have enough fighters or weapons to beat the Germans. Their fight had become more about dying an honourable death, and sending a message to the rest of the world about what was happening to them, which they hoped would be heard.

The Żydowska Organizacja Bojowa (ŻOB), the Jewish Fighting Organisation, was formed on 28 July 1942, six days after the Germans under SS General Jurgen Stroop had begun *Grossaktion Warschau*. The Żydowski Związek Wojskowy (ŻZW), the Jewish Military Union, consisting mostly of Polish Jewish officers, had been formed in 1939. Another organisation, known as the Żagiew, was in collaboration with the Germans. Also collaborationist were the *Judische Ghetto-Polizei*, auxiliary police units who policed the ghetto, but not for the benefit of the Jewish community. They were not armed, but were allowed to carry batons, and they were primarily used for helping the Germans round up other Jews for

Arm band worn by the Jewish ghetto police, Warsaw ghetto.

deportation to the concentration camps, and for any public order within the ghetto.

The German authorities spread the rumour that the liquidation of the Jews in the Warsaw ghetto would begin in April 1942. This date was subsequently changed to June. Himmler made a second visit to Warsaw in July 1942. This became the signal for the commencement of the liquidation of the Jews in the ghetto, which began on 17 July 1942, but before it did there was a registration of all foreign Jews confined there. Once they had been registered, they were removed and sent to the city's Pawiak prison. It is estimated that 300,000 men and women passed through the prison during the war. Of these, approximately 37,000 were executed at the prison, while a further 60,000 were sent to concentration camps, although exact numbers are not known as the prison's archives have never been located.

From 20 July, the guarding of the ghetto was entrusted to special security battalions formed from some less desirable types from several Eastern European countries. Large numbers of German police, armed with machine guns, were positioned at all the gates leading into the ghetto, while mobile German police detachments patrolled its boundaries day and night.

Adam Czerniakow was an engineer by profession but inside the Warsaw ghetto he was the head of the *Judenrat*. One of the Judenrat's responsibilities, along with the help of the Jewish Ghetto Police, was to provide the German authorities with lists of Jews and to draw maps showing where they lived.

At 11 am on 21 July, police cars drove into the ghetto to visit with the members of the Jewish Council at their allocated building in Grzybowska Street. The SS officers ordered Mr Czerniakow to summon the rest of the council members. On their arrival they were duly arrested by the SS officers and driven to the city's Pawiak prison. After a few hours, nearly all of them were allowed to return to the ghetto. Meanwhile, squads of police entered the ghetto and broke into houses in search of Jewish intellectuals. Anyone who was well dressed was shot dead on the spot, without the police even first bothering to identify them. Among those killed was Professor Dr Raszeja, who was not Jewish but was simply visiting the ghetto in the course of his medical duties, and he was in possession of an

Ghetto police on parade in the Warsaw ghetto (1942).

official pass. By the time the police had left the ghetto, hundreds of educated and well-off Jews had been shot dead.

The following morning, police again visited the ghetto and summoned all of the members of the Jewish Council. They were informed that an order had been issued for the removal of the entire Jewish population of the Warsaw ghetto, and printed instructions to that effect were issued in the form of posters. The number of people to be removed was fixed at 6,000 per day. They were to assemble in the hospital wards and grounds in Stawki Street:

Jewish Council in Warsaw
Notice
Warsaw, July 22nd, 1942

(1) By order of the German authorities all Jews living in Warsaw, without regard to age or sex, are to be deported to the East.

(2) The following are exempted from the deportation order:-

　(a) All Jews employed by the German authorities or German enterprises, who can produce adequate evidence of the fact.

　(b) All Jews who are members and employees of the Jewish Council according to their status on the day of publication of this order.

　(c) All Jews employed in German-owned firms who can produce adequate evidence of the fact.

　(d) All Jews not yet thus employed, but who are capable of work. These are to be barracked in the Jewish Quarter.

　(e) All Jews belonging to the Jewish civil police.

　(f) All Jews belonging to the staffs of Jewish hospitals, or belonging to Jewish disinfection squads.

　(g) All Jews who are members of the families of persons covered by (a) to (f). Only wives and children are regarded as members of families.

　(h) All Jews who on the day of deportation are patients in one of the Jewish hospitals, unless fit to be discharged. Unfitness for discharge must be attested by a doctor appointed by the Jewish Council.

(3) *Each Jew to be deported is entitled to take with him on the journey 15 kg of his personal effects. Anything in excess of 15 kg will be confiscated. All articles of value such as money, jewellery, gold, etc., may be retained. Sufficient food for three days' journey should be taken.*

(4) *Deportation begins on July 22nd, 1942, at 11 am.*

(5) *Punishments:*

    (a) *Any Jew who is not included among persons specified under par. 2 points (a) and (c) and so far not entitled to be so included, who leaves the Jewish quarter after the deportation has begun, will be shot.*

    (b) *Any Jew who undertakes activities likely to frustrate or hinder the execution of the deportation orders will be shot.*

    (c) *Any Jew who assists in any activity which might frustrate or hinder the execution of the deportation orders will be shot.*

    (d) *Any Jew found in Warsaw, after the conclusion of the deportation of Jews, who is not included among the persons specified under par. 2 points (a) to (h) will be shot.*

The part of the order that stipulated that Jews employed by German businesses would be exempt from the deportations caused competition to secure employment in one of those business. If employment could not be obtained, people would purchase fake certificates. Large sums of money were paid to obtain one. Sometimes such a certificate was useless, whether real or fake, because to make up the required numbers for deportation, police simply gathered people up off of the streets.

Czerniakow tried to obtain exemptions, including for the children in the Korczak orphanage, but he failed. At 7 pm on 23 July 1942, police officers went to the office of Mr Czerniakow. He was informed that the following day 10,000 people were required for deportation, and after that the number would be 7,000 people per day. After the police officers left, Czerniakow committed suicide. Czerniakow's wife was executed as a punishment when deportation quotas were not been met.

Without any delay Mr Czerniakow was replaced as the chairman of the Jewish Council by Mr Lichtenbaum, and the following day, 10,000 people were ready and waiting for deportation, and in the following days 7,000 people were found for each day's deportation. Mr Lichtenbaum and his colleagues on the Jewish Council proved effective in their application of the German order, and simply gathered people up in the streets or had them taken from their homes.

The deportations from the Warsaw ghetto were interrupted for five days between 20 and 25 August 1942 while the machinery for the mass slaughter of Jews was deployed on the liquidation of other ghettos in central Poland, including Falenica, Rembertow, Nowy, Dwor, Kaluszyn and Minsk Mazowiecki.

Among the deported were the youngsters from Jewish schools, orphanages and children's homes. These included the children from the orphanage of the celebrated Polish educationalist Dr Janusz Korczak, who refused to abandon his charges even though he was given the opportunity to remain behind. Instead he stayed with them and together they all perished at Treblinka on or around 7 August 1942.

Over time the deportations became more and more brutal. Each day at the allotted hour, police would enter the ghetto, cordon off the block of houses or flats which had been selected for clearance, and fire their weapons at random, this being the signal for those within to leave and assemble in the yard. Anybody attempting to escape or hide was shot dead. There was no attempt to keep families together. Wives were torn from their husbands, and children from their parents. Those who were frail or infirm were taken directly to the Jewish cemetery, killed and buried straight away. On average, 100 people per day were killed for this reason.

Once the required number of people for deportation had been gathered, they were marched to the railway station and tightly packed into cattle trucks, 120 in each. Once loaded, the trucks were locked and sealed. The floors of the trucks had been covered in a mixture of quicklime and chlorine, and many did not survive the journey.

The monument in Warsaw dedicated to Januska Korczak.

Chapter 6

Reinhard Heydrich

Reinhard Tristan Eugen Heydrich was born in 1904 in Halle an der Saale, in Saxony-Anhalt. His father was a well-known composer and opera singer, his mother was a fine pianist. Young Reinhard played the violin more than adequately.

At school he was shy and bullied because of his high-pitched voice, and because it was suspected that there might be a Jewish connection somewhere in the family, mainly based on the fact that he had a rather pronounced nose. His father also 'had the physical appearance of a Jew'.

He married Lina von Osten in 1931, who later said that Heydrich was vain and had an inferiority complex, and was not a man to show affection or tenderness, even to his wife.

After the end of the First World War there was civil unrest across Germany as communist and anti-communist groups struggled to gain political power across the beleaguered nation. Some of these clashes took place in Heydrich's home town of Halle. Then, aged 15, he joined a right-wing paramilitary Freikorps

Reinhard Heydrich: one of the chief architects of the Holocaust.

unit known as the Maercker Volunteer Rifles. He later joined the *Deutschvolkischer Schutz und Trutzbund*, or The National German Protection and Shelter League, an anti-semitic organisation.

In 1922 he enlisted in the navy but was dismissed in April 1931 for 'conduct unbecoming to an officer and a gentleman' for breaking a promise to marry a woman whom he had known for six months. He then went to Hamburg and enlisted in the Nazi Party, and on 14 July 1931 became an Untersturmführer in the SS. In the same year, Himmler, leader of the SS, had decided to set up a counter-intelligence wing of the organisation, and on the recommendation of a trusted friend and associate, Karl von Eberstein, Himmler interviewed Heydrich, and was so impressed with him that he hired him on the spot as the chief of his new Secret Intelligence Service.

In 1932, rumours that had been spread by Heydrich's enemies inside the Nazi Party questioning his ancestry again came to the surface. The allegations were investigated by the Party and dismissed. The ploy to dethrone Heydrich had not only failed, but had also greatly strengthened his position in the Nazi Party.

The Gestapo, the *Geheime Staatspolitzei*, was formed by Hermann Göring in 1933, and on 22 April 1934 Heydrich was made its head. He remained Director of the Gestapo until 27 September 1939. He was made Director of the Head Office of Reich Security on 27 September, became President of the International Criminal Police Commission on 24 August 1940 and was appointed Deputy Protector of Bohemia and Moravia on 29 September 1941. All three posts he held until his death on 4 June 1942.

He was one of the main protagonists of the Final Solution to the Jewish Question and the Holocaust. Hitler once described him as 'the man with the iron heart'. Heydrich was one of the most feared and disliked senior figures in the Nazi party.

While on his way to work in Prague, Heydrich was ambushed and fatally wounded on 27 May 1942. He died of his wounds a week later. The attackers had been sent by the Czech government in exile in London and had been trained by Britain's Special Operations Executive, SOE.

The idea behind the operation came from the head of the Czechoslovakian Intelligence Service, Frantisek Moravec. Knowing the likely repercussions, Czech resistance leaders pleaded with their government to abandon the attack, but Czechoslovakian head of state Edvard Benes still gave order to go ahead and kill Heydrich.

Jozef Gabčík, Jan Kubiš, and Josef Valčík, and several other soldiers from the Czech Army in exile took off from RAF Tangmere on the evening of 28 December 1941 and landed just east of Prague in the early hours of the following morning. They discovered the route that Heydrich took every day from his home in the village of Panenske Brezany to his office at SS headquarters at Prague castle. Heydrich took the same route every day, and had no security detail, maybe because he believed that no-one would dare to attack him. They chose a tight curve in the road for the place of the attack, close to Prague's Bulovka hospital, as Heydrich's car would have to slow considerably. Things didn't quite go according to plan. As Heydrich's open-topped Mercedes 320 convertible slowed, Gabčík stepped into the road and prepared to fire his Sten gun, but it jammed. Heydrich's driver brought the car to a halt as he was ordered, and Heydrich stood up and fired at Gabčík, but missed. As he did so Kubis threw a briefcase at the rear of the car containing a modified anti-tank grenade. It exploded and Heydrich was struck by shrapnel. He didn't appear to realise how badly injured he was and engaged in a gun battle with his two assailants. Kubiš jumped on a bicycle to escape, and Heydrich chased him on foot, Luger in hand. In the meantime Heydrich's driver chased after Gabčík, and was shot twice in the leg.

Heydrich was taken to the nearby hospital where, on being examined by both Czechoslovakian and German doctors, it was discovered that shrapnel had damaged his diaphragm, spleen and lung, and fractured one of his ribs. He appeared to be recovering well from his injuries, but a week later had a relapse, slipped into a coma and died.

After Heydrich's death the Nazis claimed that those responsible for the attack had come from the villages of Lidice and Lezaky, but they hadn't. They killed every male in the villages over the age of

16, and nearly all of the women and girls were deported to German death camps.

Heydrich's killing was the only state sponsored targeted assassination of a top Nazi member throughout the whole war, or at least the only one that was successful.

As for Valčík, Gabčík and Kubiš, it did not end well. They were betrayed by one of their own, Karel Čurda, a soldier of the Czechoslovak Army in exile, who had parachuted in to the country in 1942 to work with the Czech resistance group. Čurda was captured after the war, tried for treason, found guilty, and hanged on 29 April 1947.

Chapter 7

Einsatzgruppen

The *Einsatzgruppen*, formed in 1939, were SS paramilitary mobile death squads. They killed an estimated one million Jews, and tens of thousands of partisans, Romani people, people with disabilities, Slavs and homosexuals.

In Poland they killed many educated individuals, members of the priesthood, and the cultural elite of the country. They played an integral part in the implementation of the *Endlösung der Judenfrage,* the Final Solution to the Jewish Problem. Nearly all of the people they killed were civilians.

A member of Einsatzgruppe D takes aim during the massacre at Vinnytsia, Ukraine 1941.

Two of their more infamous mass murders were at Babi Yar, where 33,771 Jews were killed by shooting in two days, and at Rumbula where an estimated 25,000 Jews were murdered by shooting, again in two days. As the German Army moved into Russia, they killed Soviet political commissars and others.

Babi Yar is in Kiev, which in 1941 was in the Soviet Union. The decision to carry out the massacre was taken by Major General Kurt Eberhard, military governor of Kiev, Obergruppenführer Friedrich Jeckein and Commander Otto Rasch of Einsatzgruppe C. The massacre was carried out by soldiers of Sonderkommando 4a, the Sicherheitsdienst, the SD, and SS police battalions backed by the Ukrainian Auxiliary Police.

The Rumbula massacre took place in the Rumbula forest near Riga on 30 November and 8 December 1941. The dead were Latvian Jews from the Riga ghetto and 1,000 German Jews who had been transported there by train. It was carried out by Einsatzgruppe A and the Arajs Kommando, a unit of the Latvian Auxiliary Police, with

the support of other Latvian auxiliaries. In charge of the massacre was Friedrich Jeckein, who had overseen the massacre at Babi Yar two months earlier. Rudolf Lange, commander of the secret police in Riga, was also involved, and would later participate in the Wannsee Conference on 20 January 1942.

Herberts Cukurs was a member of the Arajs Kommando. He was one of those responsible for clearing the Jews out of the Riga ghetto and fired into the crowds of Latvian Jews during the Rumbula massacre. Though there were eyewitness accounts linking him to that massacre, and reports of him having been involved in other murders of civilians, he never stood trial.

After the war, Cukurs emigrated to Brazil. His visa for permanent residency was issued

Herbert Cukurs was one of those responsible for clearing the Riga ghetto.

in December 1945 by the Brazilian Embassy in Marseilles. Having settled in Brazil he started up a company, using his real name, flying aircraft for tourists on scenic flights. On 23 February 1965, aged 64, he travelled to Uruguay to meet a man using the name of Anton Kunzle who he was going to go into business with, or so he thought. Kunzle was in fact Yaakov Meidad, a Mossad agent. At the meeting, in a house in Montevideo, he was set upon by Mossad agents and shot in the head at close range. His body was found in a trunk on 6 March 1965, with several gunshot wounds and a shattered skull.

Messages arrived at news networks:

Taking into consideration the gravity of the charge levelled against the accused, namely that he personally supervised the killing of more than 30,000 men, women and children, and considering the extreme display of cruelty which the subject showed when carrying out his tasks, the accused, Herbert Cukurs, is hereby sentenced to death. Accused was executed by those who can never forget, on 23 February 1965. His body can be found at Casa Cubertini, Calle Colombia, Septima Seccion del Departamento de Canelones, Montevideo, Uruguay.

After the war the Einsatzgruppen had their own trial, which took place between 29 September 1947 and 10 April 1948. The three charges in all cases were for crimes against humanity, war crimes, and membership of a criminal organisation. Both the SS and the Gestapo had also been declared criminal organisations at the Nuremberg Military Tribunals. The trials were all held before United States military courts, and not before the International Military Tribunal. There were twenty-four defendants, all officers. They all pleaded not guilty.

Ernst Biberstein had studied theology and became a priest in 1924. He was commanding officer of Sonderkommando 6 of Einsatzgruppe C. He had been present at and also supervised killings at different times throughout the war. Found guilty, he was sentenced to death by hanging, which was commuted to life imprisonment in 1951. He was released in 1958 and died in 1986.

Paul Blobel was commanding officer of Sonderkommando 4a of Einsatzgruppe C. He was sentenced to death by hanging, and was executed on 7 June 1951. In August 1941 he was put in charge of creating a ghetto in the Ukrainian city of Zhytomyr, which resulted in the murder of 3,000 Jews. Later that same month he was also involved in the massacre at Bila Tserkva, when the entire Jewish adult population were murdered. Ninety children were later found hiding; they were taken to a mass grave that had already been dug, and shot. Blobel was one of the main figures involved in the Babi Yar massacre in 1941. In June 1942 he was in charge of Sonderaktion 1005, who were tasked with hiding evidence of mass murders by the Nazis in Poland and Eastern Europe. This involved the exhumation and burning of thousands of dead bodies.

Walter Blume was commanding officer of Sonderkommando 7a of Einsatzgruppe B. He was captured by the Americans in Salzburg and sent to Landsberg prison in Bavaria. He was found guilty of having committed atrocities against the Jews in Belarus and Russia, as well as sending 46,000 Jews to Auschwitz from Greece. He was sentenced to death by hanging, subsequently commuted to twenty-five years, and was released in 1955. He was rearrested in 1968 in relation to the deportation of Jews from Greece. Despite the considerable evidence against him, all charges were dropped on 29 January 1971. In 1997, a relative, Albert Blume, had a pawnbroking business in Brazil. He was found in possession of gold bars, gold teeth, luxury watches, and rings, along with military identity documents in the name of Colonel Walter Blume. The value of the cache in 1997 was estimated at $4 million.

Werner Braune had commanded Sonderkommando 11b Einsatzgruppe D. He organised and conducted mass executions of Jews at Simferopol in the Crimea between 11 and 13 December 1941, during which time 14,300 Jews were murdered. He was found guilty and sentenced to death. He was hanged on 7 June 1951 at Landsberg prison.

Lothar Fendler was deputy chief of Sonderkommando 4b and Einsatzgruppe C. He was found guilty and sentenced to ten years imprisonment, which was reduced to eight in 1951. The reason behind the reduction of some of the sentences was in part the outbreak of the Korean war in 1950, and the rearmament of the newly formed West Germany. Fendler claimed that his role was intelligence officer and that he wrote reports on the morale of the local population. The case against him focused on whether he reported directly to Gunther Herrmann, which was not proved.

Matthias Graf was an officer in Einsatzkommando 6 of Einsatzgruppe D. He was found guilty of membership of the SD, the intelligence agency of the SS. He had in fact been expelled from the SS for 'general indifference to the organisation'. He later even tried to be relieved from the SD. He was released at the end of the trial, his punishment being time served. He was dealt with so leniently because he was a non-commissioned officer, had never held any command position, and had even refused the opportunity to become an officer.

Walter Haensch was commanding officer of Sonderkommando 4b of Einsatzgruppe C. He was found guilty as charged and sentenced to death by hanging. This was commuted to fifteen years imprisonment in 1951.

Emil Haussmann was an officer in Einsatzkommando 12 of Einsatzgruppe D, which carried out the murders of an estimated one million Jews during the German occupation of South Ukraine between 1941 and 1944. At the end of the war he was arrested by Allied troops in Poland and sent to Landsberg prison. He committed suicide in his cell two days after being given the indictment that he was to be charged.

Heinz Jost was commanding officer of Einsatzgruppe A. He was sentenced to life imprisonment, later commuted to ten years, and he was released in 1951. He died in 1964.

Waldemar Klingelhöfer was an officer of Sonderkommando 7b of Einsatzgruppe B. He was found guilty and sentenced to death. This was later commuted to life imprisonment and he was released in 1956. In 1960 it was known that he was working as a clerk in Villingen. He died in 1980 at the age of 80. Klingelhöfer was born in Moscow in 1900, and before the war was an opera singer. At his trial he claimed that he was only an interpreter in the Einsatzgruppe.

By November 1941 Einsatzgruppe B had been responsible for an estimated 45,000 murders, and evidence was produced in court to show that Klingelhöfer had been present when executions had taken place, and that on one occasion he personally shot thirty Jews who had left a ghetto without permission.

Erich Naumann was commanding officer of Einsatzgruppe B. He sent reports to Eichmann in November 1941 that his unit was responsible for the deaths of 17,256 Jews in Smolensk. He admitted that his unit had possessed three gas vans which 'were used to exterminate human beings'. He was sentenced to death, and hanged on 7 June 1951.

Gustav Adolf Nosske was a commanding officer in Einsatzkommando 12 of Einsatzgruppe D. In August 1941 he and his men were tasked with moving 11,000 Jews from Yampil in Western Ukraine to the Romanian zone on the other side of the Dniester River. During the march, hundreds of the Jews were murdered, and between 16 and 28 February 1942 Nosske and his men were responsible for the deaths of 1,499 civilians, including Jews, communists, partisans and Romani. He was found guilty and sentenced to life imprisonment, which in 1951 was commuted to ten years' imprisonment, and he was released in 1955. He died in 1990 aged 87.

Otto Ohlendorf was commanding officer of Einsatzgruppe D. He was sentenced to death by hanging and executed on 7 June 1951.

Adolf Ott was commanding officer of Sonderkommando 7b of Einsatzgruppe B. He was found guilty of all charges against him and sentenced to death by hanging, but this was commuted to life imprisonment, and he was released from Landsberg on 9 May 1958.

Otto Rasch was commanding officer of Einsatzgruppe C. He was removed from the trial on 5 February 1948 due to health reasons, and died on 1 November 1948.

Felix Ruhl was an officer of Sonderkommando 10b of Einsatzgruppe D. He was found not guilty of counts 1 and 2 against him, but guilty of the third charge, being a member of a criminal organisation, for which he was sentenced to ten years imprisonment, which he served in its entirety. The court decided that, as a subaltern officer, he was not responsible for the atrocities that had been committed by Einsatzgruppe D and was in no position to prevent them. It also felt that although he knew of the killings, it could not be proved that he personally took part in them.

Martin Sandberger was commanding officer of Sonderkommando 1a of Einsatzgruppe A. He was responsible for the arrest and deportation to Auschwitz of thousands of Jews from Italy, and the mass murder of Jews in the Baltic States. He was also the commander of the SS in Estonia. He was sentenced to death by hanging, later commuted to life imprisonment, and he was released in 1958. He died aged 98 on 30 March 2010 in Stuttgart.

Heinze Schubert was an officer in Einsatzgruppe D. In December 1941 he was given orders to organise the killing of about 800 people in Simperfol in the Crimea, which he did. He was found guilty on all counts and sentenced to death by hanging. The sentence was commuted to ten years' imprisonment. He served just four years.

Erwin Schultz was commanding officer of Einsatzkommando 5 of Einsatzgruppe C. He was sentenced to twenty years in imprisonment, commuted to fifteen. He was released from prison on 9 January 1954 and died in 1981.

Willie Siebert was deputy chief of Einsatzgruppe D. He was found guilty on all three charges and sentenced to death. This was later commuted to fifteen years' imprisonment.

Franz Six was commanding officer of the Vorkommando Moscow of Einsatzgruppe B. He was sentenced to twenty years, subsequently reduced to fifteen, and he was released on 30 September 1952. He died in 1975. In 1941 Heydrich had asked Six to plan the elimination of anti-Nazi elements in Britain.

Eugen Steimle was was commanding officer of Sonderkommando 7a of Einsatzgruppe B between 7 September and 10 December 1941. In that time they were responsible for the deaths of some 500 Jews. Between August 1942 and January 1943 he became the commanding officer of Sonderkommando 4a of Einsatzgruppe C, also responsible for numerous mass murders in the Soviet Union. He was found guilty on all three charges and was sentenced to death. This was commuted to twenty years in prison, and he was released in June 1954. After his release he returned to his civilian profession of teaching. He died on 9 October 1987 aged 77.

Eduard Strauch was commanding officer of Einsatzkommando 2 of Einsatzgruppe A and went on to become a senior officer in the Security Police and the SD, serving in Belarus and Belgium before ending up in the military branch of the Waffen-SS. On 30 November 1941, along with some twenty of his men, he was involved in the murder of 10,600 Jews in Rumbula forest. In July 1943 he was congratulated by the Nazi General Commissioner for White Russia for having caused 'the liquidation of 55,000 Jews in just the past ten weeks alone'. SS Obergruppenführer Erich von dem Bach-Zelewski, who was himself involved in the Holocaust, described Strauch as 'the worst human I ever met in my life'. At his arraignment on 15 September 1947, Strauch had an epileptic fit. His defence team tried to have him removed from the case because of poor health. This was refused by the members of the tribunal, who had noted his demeanour and commented that he gave his testimonies to the court coherently and in a way which gave no concern about his mental capability to stand trial or prevented him from understanding the court proceedings. Despite his attempts to pretend to be suffering from mental illness, he was found guilty of all three charges and sentenced to death by hanging, but Staunch was not hanged; instead he was handed over to the Belgian authorities to be tried for war crimes he had committed in their country. Once again he was found guilty, and sentenced to death by hanging. While held in Belgian custody he died in hospital on 15 September 1955, having managed to escape the hangman's noose for a second time.

Waldemar von Radetzky was deputy chief of Sonderkommando 4a of Einsatzgruppe C, and was sentenced to twenty years imprisonment. He was released in 1951.

Chapter 8

Auschwitz

I visited Auschwitz I and Auschwitz II-Birkenau camps in the spring of 2005, the year of the sixtieth anniversary of the camps' liberation by American forces. While there, in company with my wife, I was spat and shouted at by a small group of people in a language that I did not recognize. The only conclusion I could sensibly come to as to why this had happened was that my physical appearance

Auchwitz II-Birkenau.

had made them believe I was a German who possibly held certain political beliefs. I am over 6 feet tall, weigh about 17 stone, have tattoos on both forearms, and at the time I had a shaved head and a goatee beard. It would be fair to say that my appearance looked somewhat thuggish.

There was an eeriness to both camps and a strange feeling of treading in the footsteps of those who had been murdered there by the Nazis. My lasting memory of the visit was more connected to Auschwitz II-Birkenau. While there I went up into the tower which sits immediately above the camp's main railway entrance. It was a surreal moment. I flicked through the pages of a book on the camp I had purchased that morning and came across a photograph which had been taken from roughly the spot where I was standing, some sixty years before. It was of a train which had arrived at the camp, and those who had been travelling on it had just emptied out on to the makeshift platform. I looked into the camp to roughly the same spot, which was about 150 yards away from where I was standing. All these years later there was no train, no platform, and no large group of people, but using one of the huts as a marker, I was able to work out the location of the photograph. The people in the picture had more than likely been killed in less time than I had spent up in the tower. I glanced at the photograph again, and then back at the same spot in the camp. I did this so many times that the two almost became blurred into one. Momentarily, it all became alive and so very real.

From the tower I made my way into the camp. It was an experience that put life in perspective. As I recall, there wasn't much in the way of talking. Such a place almost doesn't need words, just personal reflection and thoughts of how fortunate we were to have been born in a different time and place.

Prisoner accommodation at Birkenau was in large wooden sheds, with wooden bunks running along both sides. They looked far from comfortable, and in the middle of a harsh Polish winter, the sheds wouldn't have offered too much in the way of protection against the weather.

The entrance to Auschwitz, showing the infamous 'Arbeit Macht Frei' *gates.*

Auschwitz was named after the Polish village of Monowice where it was built. The Germans used their own spelling: Monowitz. Auschwitz I was a concentration camp, Auschwitz II was a concentration and extermination camp, Auschwitz III was a concentration and labour camp.

The following is an excerpt from the explanation of jury decisions in the first Auschwitz trial:

Torturing of prisoners [of Auschwitz] *already tormented to the extreme* [by extrajudicial means] *is the evidence of inhuman savagery perpetrated by those defendants who as a result of the trial were sentenced to death. The listed violent crimes committed by named defendants, who all took smaller or larger parts in the mass murder of prisoners, also reveal that the accused were involved in the acts of killing for pleasure, and not pursuant to orders of their superiors. If it were not for their expressed desire to kill, they would have otherwise displayed elements of sympathy for the victims, or at least shown indifference to their plight, but not torture them to death.*

Rudolf Höss

Auschwitz had three commandants during its time as a concentration camp. The first was Rudolf Höss, who was commandant on two occasions: from 4 May 1940 to November 1943 and again from 8 May 1944 to 18 January 1945.

During Höss's first spell, it was his deputy, Karl Fritzch, who came up with the idea of using Zyklon B (hydrogen-cyanide) to kill en masse. It was first used in August 1941 when Fritzch, acting as commandant in the absence of Höss, ordered the killing of Russian prisoners of war who were locked in their air-tight cells.

There is an interesting story behind why there was a break in Höss's time as commandant at Auschwitz. In 1942 he is reported to have had an affair with a non-Jewish female inmate of Auschwitz. She was at the camp as a political prisoner and went by the name of either Eleonore or Nora Hodys. During the affair she became pregnant with Höss's child. When Hodys informed him that she was pregnant, he didn't have her killed as one might have expected, or force her to have an abortion, instead he had her imprisoned at Auschwitz in a standing-only arrest cell. The camp had four of these cells, which were located in the basement of Block 11. I saw them on my visit to Auschwitz in 2005 and there was literally just enough room to stand. Later she had an abortion in the camp's hospital. One assumes this was something about which she had no choice. She survived to be released from captivity in 1944 and give evidence against Höss, but was killed by the SS before the end of the war. Höss was replaced as commandant on 10 November 1943, possibly as a result of this affair, but six months later, on 8 May 1944, he returned to the camp as its commandant. This coincided with the arrival of 430,000 Hungarian Jews, and in just 56 days, between May and July 1944, every single one of them had been killed in the camp's gas chambers.

Höss was a married man. He lived with his wife and five children in a large detached house that backed onto the camp. During the day he was a mass murderer and in the evening he made the short journey back to his home where he was a loving husband and father.

After the war, Höss and his family fled north with the intention of escaping to South America. He remained at large for nearly a year before he was discovered in Gottrupel in Germany and was arrested. British soldiers turned up at their 'home' and started beating up their 16-year-old son, Laus. Höss's wife Hedwig then told them where to find him. He was pretending to be a gardener, calling himself Franz Lang. Captain Hanns Alexander of the British Army ordered him to take off his wedding ring, which he reluctantly did, and the game was up, as the name Rudolph Höss was inscribed on the inside. Alexander was actually German, having been born in Berlin, but in 1936, aged 19, he fled to England with his parents and siblings, who were all Jewish. In 1940 he joined the Royal Pioneer Corps, and in 1945 he joined the No.1 War Crimes Investigation Team at Belsen as an interpreter.

Höss's middle child, Inge-Brigitt, married an American. She had two children and spent thirty-five years working in a Jewish-owned fashion boutique in Washington, D.C.

Höss appeared before the International Military Tribunal at Nuremberg on 15 April 1946, having already confessed his crimes:

I commanded Auschwitz until 1 December 1943, and estimate that at least 2,500,000 victims were executed and exterminated there by gassing and burning, and at least another half a million succumbed to starvation and disease, making a total of about 3,000,000 dead. This figure represents about 70 or 80 per cent of all persons sent to Auschwitz as prisoners, the remainder having been selected and used for slave labour in the concentration camp industries. Included among the executed and burnt were approximately 20,000 Russian prisoners of war, who had previously been screened out of Prisoner of War cages by the Gestapo, and then delivered to Auschwitz in Wehrmacht transports operated by regular Wehrmacht officers and men. The remainder of the total number of victims included about 100,000 German Jews, and great numbers of citizens, mostly Jewish from the Netherlands, France, Belgium, Poland,

Hungary, Czechoslovakia, Greece or other countries. We executed about 400,000 Hungarian Jews alone at Auschwitz in the summer of 1944.

On 25 May 1946, Höss was handed over to the Polish authorities and put before their Supreme National Tribunal, where he was tried. While in custody in Krakow he wrote an essay about Auschwitz: 'I myself never knew the total number [who died there], and I have nothing to help me arrive at an estimate. I can only remember the figures involved in the larger actions, which were repeated to me by Eichmann or his deputies.' His notes included a list of countries and the number of Jews who had been deported to Auschwitz from each. By now his estimate of the number of Jews who arrived at Auschwitz and been murdered had reduced to 1,130,000. Murdered was not a word that he used: 'I can no longer remember the figures for the smaller actions, but they

Hungarian Jews arriving at Auschwitz, May 1941.

Hungarian Jews going through 'Selection' at Auschwitz II-Birkenau.

were insignificant by comparison with the numbers given above. I regard a figure of 2.5 million as far too high. Even Auschwitz had limits to its destructive capabilities.'

French scholar George Wellers in 1983, using German data on deportations, suggests that the number killed at Auschwitz was 1,471,595; and Franciszek Piper, a Polish author, historian and scholar, came up with a figure of 1,500,000 by using train timetables and deportation records.

Höss was found guilty and sentenced to death by hanging. In what must have been a considered decision, his execution took place

Rudolf Höss moments before he was hanged at Auschwitz, 1947.

on 16 April in the grounds of Auschwitz I concentration camp, immediately between one of the crematoriums and his old home where he had lived with his wife and children while commandant.

Arthur Liebenhenschel

Obersturmbannführer Arthur Liebenhenschel was commandant at Auschwitz I for the six months that Rudolph Höss was relieved of his command, between 1 December 1943 and 8 May 1944. Life under him was no better for those held at Auschwitz than it had been under Höss. The mass executions still continued, although he did do away with the four standing cells and ended the gassing of non-Jewish prisoners.

After Auschwitz, Liebehenschel was sent to take command of Majdanek camp. By the time he arrived there on 19 May 1944, there were no prisoners, as they had all been evacuated following the arrival of the Red Army. Two months later, on 22 July, he was transferred to Trieste where he was made head of the SS Manpower Office.

Arthur Liebehenschel took over from Rudolf Höss as commandant at Auschwitz.

After the war Liebehenschel was arrested by the US Army and sent back to Poland where he was tried by the Polish Supreme National Tribunal. He was found guilty, sentenced to death, and hanged on 24 January 1948 in Krakow.

Including Liebehenschel, there were forty former Auschwitz staff on trial. Only one, Doctor Hans Wilhelm Munch, was acquitted. He had been a doctor at Auschwitz between 1943 and 1945. Twenty-three were sentenced to death, two of whom had their sentences commuted to life imprisonment. Six were sentenced to life imprisonment, seven were sentenced to fifteen years, one was sentenced to ten years, one five years, and another three years.

Amongst the defendants were women guards. Maria Mandel is mentioned elsewhere in this book in more detail; Therese Brandl; Luise Danz was initially sentenced to life imprisonment but was released after just ten under a general amnesty of the Polish authorities; Hildegard Lachert and Alice Orlowski. The two latter were horrible creatures whose brutality and enjoyment of what they did was almost unprecedented, but Lachert went on to be employed by both the West German spy Agency *Bundesnachrichtendiest*, the Federal Intelligence Service, the BND, and the American CIA.

Hildegard Martha Lachert was a nurse. In 1942 she was called up to serve as a camp guard, initially at Majdanek, where she remained until 1944. After she returned to work having given birth to her third child, she was sent to work at Auschwitz, where she gained a reputation for being sadistic in the extremes: 'the worst of the worst' was one way she was described. She is also believed to have served at the Bolzano camp in northern Italy and at the Mauthausen-Gusen camp in Austria. At Auschwitz she was said to have taken to her role of selecting those to be sent to the gas chamber with consummate ease. Her party trick was setting her dog onto inmates and revel in the pain that was caused. In November 1947 she appeared in the Krakow court room, in company with forty other SS (including Alice Orlowski, Therese Brandt, and Luise Danz), to stand trial. Lachert was sentenced to fifteen years imprisonment but ended up serving only nine.

But that wasn't to be the end of the matter. In 1975, the West German government decided to try sixteen women who had been guards at the Majdanek concentration camp. Lachert was one. Two others were Alice Orlowski and Hermine Braunsteiner, who had to be extradited from the United States. The case, held in Düssledorf, took nearly six years, during which time Lachert was held in custody. Her sadistic nature was referred to time and time again by the witnesses. She was sentenced to twelve years imprisonment, but because she had already spent nine years in custody in Poland, and another five in West Germany, she was dealt with by way of time served. She died in Berlin in 1995, aged 75.

Work on Auschwitz II-Birkenau began in October 1941 as an overflow to Auschwitz I, to house 50,000 prisoners of war who would be used as labourers. It was intended to allow expansion up to a possible 200,000 inmates. In October 1941 some 10,000 Russian prisoners of war arrived at Auschwitz I, but by March the following year less than 1,000 were still alive. By this time the Nazis had decided on the Final Solution, so the ideas about Auschwitz II-Birkenau had changed. It was no longer going to be a prisoner of war camp, instead it was to be used as a labour and extermination camp, mainly for Jewish people.

The new camp had four crematoria, a reception building, and many accommodation blocks. All the crematoria were up and running by June 1943.

Karl Bischoff, who was neither a soldier nor an SS officer, was the architect. Bischoff was not charged with any offences at Nuremberg.

Besides these three main camps there were forty-four other sub-camps which came under the heading of Auschwitz, established between December 1941 and December 1944, holding anything between 20 and 10,000 inmates each.

Bauzug, for example, located near Karlsruhe, held 500 prisoners. It was unusual in that it was a train, used as the SS Main Economic and Administrative Office, and was responsible for running the

Rings taken from death camp inmates.

Oswald Pohl at the Nuremberg Trials, 1947.

Nazi party's finances, its supply systems, and business projects. It was also in charge of concentration camps. The man in charge of the office was Obergruppenführer Oswald Ludwig Pohl. Under his guidance everybody who arrived at one of the death camps had their gold and jewellery taken from them, which was then sent to the Reichsbank in Berlin.

Pohl survived the war, was captured by the Allies, and put on trial for war crimes at Nuremberg. He was found guilty and later executed at Landsberg Prison on 7 June 1952. The reason for the delay in his execution was that he appealed his conviction several times.

Josef Mengele

Nazi doctors, such as Josef Mengele, carried out numerous operations and experiments on camp inmates for no other reason than to satisfy their own warped curiosity and sadism.

Mengele was born in Günzburg, Bavaria, in 1911, the eldest of three brothers. The family was affluent, as Mengele's father was the founder of Karl Mengele & Sons, which made farm machinery.

On leaving high school at 19, he went on to study philosophy in Munich. In 1931 he joined one of the many paramilitary groups which sprung up after Germany's defeat in the First World War, the *Stahlhelm, Bund der Frontsoldaten.*

In 1935 he received a PhD in anthropology and in 1937 began working as an assistant for Dr Otmar Freiherr von Verschuer, a professor of human genetics whose main field of work was the study of twins, at the Institute for Hereditary Biology and Racial Hygiene in Frankfurt. Mengele's line of focus became the factors which resulted in cleft lips and

Doctor Josef Mengele.

palates. In 1938 he wrote a thesis on the subject and received a doctorate in medicine from the University of Frankfurt. Up to this point, Mengele appeared to have been nothing other than a respected practitioner in his chosen field.

He joined the Nazi Party in 1937 and a year later joined the SS. He was called up for military service in June 1940 and volunteered for medical service with the Waffen-SS, where he served in a reserve medical battalion until November. He was then assigned to the SS Race and Settlement Main Office in Posen (now Poznań), where he acted as a medical expert. This office supported a policy of ethnic cleansing and eventually genocide.

After seven months in Poland he was on the move again, this time to the Ukraine. Seven months after that, in January 1942, he was transferred to the 5th SS Panzer Division Wiking as a medical officer. This division was recruited from non-German volunteers but served under a German officer. While serving with them he was awarded the Iron Cross 1st Class for saving two German soldiers from a burning tank. He also received the Black Wound Badge and the Medal for the Care of German People.

In 1942 he was seriously wounded in action during fighting in the port city of Rostov-on-Don and was declared unfit for further active service. On recovery he went back to work with von Verschuer, who encouraged him in early 1943 to apply for a transfer to the concentration camp service.

Mengele's application was accepted and he was sent to work at Auschwitz, where he was given the position of chief physician to the Romani family camp, a sub-camp within the main Auschwitz II-Birkenau camp. Auschwitz had a chief medical officer, Eduard Wirths, and other Nazi doctors, who oversaw inmate doctors who were given no choice but to work in the camp's medical service.

Mengele took it upon himself to make weekly visits to the camp's hospital barracks where sick prisoners were held, and one morning ordered that prisoners were no longer allowed to spend more than two weeks in bed. Anybody who was not well enough to go back to work after that time was to be sent to the gas chambers.

Mengele volunteered himself for the selection process when new inmates arrived in the camp by train, a job that most doctors had no time for and usually did under duress, but not Mengele: he did it with a relish. For him it was an opportunity to find people who he could use to experiment on, such as twins.

Typhus had been rife at Auschwitz for some time, but the Nazis didn't really care about it until a senior SS doctor became infected with the disease and died. Doctor Mengele's remedy was to send six hundred Jewish women from an infected block to the gas chamber. The block was then cleaned and disinfected. The prisoners from an adjoining block, which had not been infected, were bathed, deloused, provided with new clothes, and moved into the clean block. This process was repeated until the entire barracks had been cleaned. For his decisive action Mengele was awarded the War Merit Cross 2nd Class with swords) and was promoted to First Physician of the Birkenau subcamp.

Auschwitz provided Mengele with the opportunity to continue his anthropological studies on a limitless supply of human beings. When he finished one experiment, he just discarded the individual, or what was left of them, and started on another.

It was rumoured that he did not always administer anaesthetic to his patients, leaving them in agony while they were being experimented on.

Mengele's old mentor, von Verschuer, requested the German Research Foundation to provide Mengele with a grant for his experimentation. This they duly did: the money was spent on a pathology laboratory where autopsies could be carried out, attached to one of the crematoria at Auschwitz II-Birkenau. Von Verschuer was sent regular reports from Mengele about his experiments. He was also sent specimens that had been harvested from his victims. Mengele had particular interest in individuals with physical abnormalities: dwarves, identical twins, and people with heterochromia iridium (eyes of different colours).

Twins supposedly enabled him to study heritable traits, with the aim of endorsing the Nazi premise of the superiority of the Aryan race. He was also interested in increasing the German population more rapidly by improving the chances of German women giving birth to twins.

One of his assistants, Doctor Miklos Nyiszil, a Hungarian Jewish pathologist who had been sent to the camp with his wife and daughter, recalled how twins were subjected to weekly examinations and measurements of their physical attributes. He described some of the experiments Mengele performed: he would, for example, amputate the limb from one child to see if this caused a reaction in the other. On one occasion he infected one twin with typhus before transfusing the blood of the infected twin into the other. Nyiszil witnessed Mengele kill fourteen pairs of twins one night by injecting their hearts with chloroform. His fascination with eyes saw him carry out some exceptionally cruel experiments. Mengele believed he could change eye colour by injecting chemicals into the eyes of a living unanaesthetised patient; most victims either went blind or died. People with heterochromatic eyes were killed and their eyes removed so that they could be sent to von Verschuer in Berlin for further study.

Most of Mengele's twins were young children. On one occasion he chose a pair of Romani child twins, sewed them together back to back, and left them to see if they would grow together and become Siamese twins. A week later they died of gangrene.

If a twin in the camp died of a disease, he would kill the other twin so that post mortems could be carried out on the pair.

With Russian forces making their way across Poland, Mengele left Auschwitz on 17 January 1945, ten days before they arrived. He then went to the concentration camp at Gross Rosen, which today is in Poland. He left there on 18 February 1945, a week before the Russians arrived.

Mengele and his unit were arrested by American forces in June 1945. He gave his real name, but remarkably he was not on the wanted list, nor did he have an SS blood group tattoo, and at the end of July he was released. Hardly able to believe his luck, he managed to acquire false papers. Using the name Fritz Hollmann, he remained on the run in Germany until July 1949 when, having acquired a passport in the name of Helmet Gregor from the International Committee of the Red Cross, he sailed for Argentina. He would live in Argentina, Paraguay and Brazil, for the next thirty years until his death on 7 February 1979. He was buried under the name of Wolfgang Gerhard.

Anne Frank

Annelies Mary Frank, better known to the world as Anne Frank, was born in Frankfurt on 12 June 1929, where she lived with her parents Otto Heinrich and Edith, and her elder sister Margot Betti. The family were Jewish, and in late 1933, soon after the Nazis came to power, Otto quickly recognised the danger he and his family would soon be in and moved them to Amsterdam. Otto had been a banker in Germany, so he was leaving a good job, but believing that he and his family were safe in neutral Holland, it was a price he was prepared to pay. But on 10 May 1940, Holland was invaded by Germany. After just four days, Dutch forces surrendered. The country's government and royal family quickly fled to London, others settled in Canada. Holland would not be free from German occupation until 8 May 1945.

Initially after the German invasion, things were not that problematic for the Franks. It was only as time went on and the Nazis began their implementation of the Final Solution, that

The memorial to Anne and Margot Frank at Bergen-Belsen.

MARGOT
FRANK
1926–1945
ANNE
FRANK
1929–1945

נר ה נשמת אדם
(SPRÜCHE 20,27)

things started becoming more dangerous for Holland's Jewish families. So it was that in July 1942, the Franks went into hiding in some concealed rooms behind a bookcase in the seventeenth-century town house where Anne Frank's father, Otto, worked as managing director of Opekta, a company which supplied pectin and spices for jam making. The house is still there, preserved, on the Prinsengracht.

Behind the bookcase the Frank family lived for more than two years, with Hermann and Auguste van Pels and their son Peter, until they were discovered and arrested on 4 August 1944 by Gestapo officer Karl Silberbauer acting on a tip-off received by his commanding officer SS Lieutenant Julius Dettmann.

Anne, as everyone knows, kept a beautifully-written diary during her incarceration. Little did she know how famous she would become after her death.

She and her sister Margot were sent to Auschwitz, and then a couple of months later to Bergen-Belsen. There are no definite dates for when Anne and Margot moved camps or when and how they died, but the Dutch authorities have officially settled on the date of 31 March 1945 as the day they died, possibly of typhus, but again, nobody knows for certain.

The only one of the Frank family to survive the holocaust was Otto. He also was sent to Auschwitz, and when the camp was liberated by Russian soldiers on 27 January 1945, he was in the camp's sick barracks. As soon as he could, he returned to his home in Amsterdam. His secretary, Hermine 'Miep' Gies, had kept Anne's diaries and gave them to Otto, who had them published in the form of a book entitled *The Diary of a Young Girl*. It remains one of the most famous chronicles of the Second World War.

The Women's Orchestra of Auschwitz

The Women's Orchestra of Auschwitz came in to being in April 1943 and was the brainchild of SS Oberaufseherin Maria Mandel. Members of the orchestra tended to be younger women and, due to it's strictly non-Jewish policy, the orchestra remained small until May 1943, when Jewish women were given permission to join.

Being selected for the orchestra was literally a life-saver. Players were treated better than other inmates, had better accommodation, received more food, and were spared the daily labour duties that ordinary prisoners had to do, mainly because they practiced for 8 hours a day, 6 days a week. The orchestra played a significant part in prison life. The last thing the work groups would hear when they left the camp in the morning, and the first thing that they would hear on their return, would be music played to them by the Auschwitz Women's Orchestra. They would also have to perform at roll-calls, selections for the gas chambers from arriving trains, camp executions, and concerts for the SS officers and men, something which they had no choice in if they wanted to carry on living. The orchestra would sometimes have to play for hours at a time, outdoors and in all weathers.

One of the conductors was Zofia Czajkowska. She was Polish, prison number 6873. When Jews were allowed to join the orchestra, Alma Rosé took over in August 1943, but Zofia continued to play violin.

Alma Rosé

Alma had married Czech violinist Váša Příhoda in 1930. Her mother's brother was the composer Gustav Mahler and her father Alfred led the Vienna Philharmonic for 50 years between 1881 and 1931 and also led the Vienna State Opera.

Alma and her father had actually escaped Nazi-occupied Austria and made their way to London. But, feeling safe, she later made her way to neutral Holland, where she hoped to continue her career. When Germany invaded and occupied the country, Alma moved to France, and then, in late 1942, when life in German-occupied France had become dangerous for an Austrian Jew, she decided to make a break for Switzerland. But she was stopped and arrested at the border by the Gestapo. In July 1943 she ended up in Auschwitz.

As soon as she arrived she became very ill, possibly with typhus, and had to be quarantined, but fortunately she made a full recovery. A somewhat dangerous pastime of Alma's was to have the orchestra play forbidden music during rehearsals, such as Chopin's beautiful Étude in E major, *Sadness*. Fortunately for her the SS guards were not too up to date on composers and their music.

Rose died suddenly on 5 April 1944, aged 36, possibly of food poisoning and was replaced by a Russian pianist, Sonia Vinogradova.

Esther Lowy

At the time of writing this book in 2019, Esther Bejarano (née Lowy) was still alive at the age of 94. A German Jew, she played the piccolo, accordion, and guitar. In 1940, aged 15, she left home and tried to emigrate to Israel but was unsuccessful. This resulted in her being arrested and serving a two-year prison sentence with hard labour in the Landwerk Neuendorf camp, near Fürstenwalde-Spree. On 23 April 1943 all of those still at the camp were sent to Auschwitz. When her musical ability was discovered she joined the Women's Orchestra, playing the accordion. She survived the war and emigrated to Israel, although she later returned to Germany, setting up home in Hamburg. Amongst her numerous achievements, she is the co-founder and chairman of the International Auschwitz Committee. The group maintains contact with survivors who live in eastern and western Europe, supports survivors of the camp, and fights racism and anti-Semitism.

Helena Dunicz-Niwińska

Another notable member of the orchestra was Helena Dunicz-Niwińska, prison number 64118. She was born in Vienna, but grew up in Lwów, in what is now the Ukraine, where she played violin with the Conservatory of the Polish Society Musical Society. When the war broke out Helena was still in Lwów with her family, where she might have felt relatively safe, but that feeling would have evaporated on 5 July 1941 when Germany began the invasion of the Ukraine. Helena and her mother were arrested in 1943 and sent to Auschwitz, where she became a member of the women's orchestra. She remained at Auschwitz II-Birkenau until January 1945, when inmates and staff were evacuated to Ravensbrück. From there she was sent on to Neustadt-Glewe, a satellite camp of Ravensbrück, where she remained until the camp was liberated in April 1945. After the war she settled in Krakow. Helena died on 12 June 2018, having lived to the age of 102.

Fania Fénelon

Fania Fénelon, whose real name was Fanja Goldstein, was a French Jewish pianist. She was born in Paris in 1908 to a Catholic mother and a Jewish father who worked as an engineer in the rubber industry. As a young girl, she studied at the Paris Conservatoire under the opera singer Germaine Martinelli during the day, and sung in bars and clubs during the evenings, into the early hours to earn money. Despite her diminutive size, she joined the French resistance in 1940, wanting to do her bit to save her country from the evil clutches of Nazi Germany. She was subsequently arrested and sent to Auschwitz, where her prison number, 74862, was tattooed onto her arm. She became a member of the women's orchestra, in which she sang, played the piano, was a drummer, and occasionally arranged music. In January 1945, she was evacuated to Bergen-Belsen where she contracted typhus. At one stage she weighed only sixty-five pounds, but she survived and was liberated by the British on 15 April 1945, when, despite her illness, she sang for the BBC on the very day of her liberation.

In 1975 she published *Sursis pour l'orchestre*, a personal record of what she had witnessed at Auschwitz and Belsen, using the diary she had kept while a prisoner. Not all of the other orchestra members agreed with everything she wrote, particularly her negative comments about Alma Rosé. What was surprising were the 'religious, cultural and national tensions and rivalries amongst the girls of the orchestra, and the anti-Semitism of some of the Polish members. It was also an intimate account, telling of prostitution and the desire for lesbian relationships.

In 1980 the American playwright Arthur Miller wrote a script for a TV film, *Playing for Time*, based on Fania Fénelon's autobiography. The film, *The Musicians of Auschwitz*, caused much controversy. Fénelon was displeased by the choice of Vanessa Redgrave to play her in the film because Redgrave was too tall at six feet, and, more importantly, because Redgrave openly criticized Zionism and had strong pro-Palestine views and opinions.

Fania Fénelon died at the age of 75 in a Paris hospital on 19 December 1983.

Anita Lasker-Wallfisch

Anita Lasker arrived at Auschwitz in December 1943 when she was 18 with her sister Renate, on separate prison trains, which were far more comfortable than the cattle trucks that most Jews arrived in. Arriving on such a train also meant that there was no selection process on arrival. She played the cello and was going to Auschwitz to be part of the Women's Orchestra.

In October 1944 Anita and her sister were part of the 3,000 who were moved by train to Bergen-Belsen. At Belsen they had very little to eat, but they survived. Renate, who could speak, read and write perfect English, began working for the British as an interpreter. As for Anita, she was sent to the Bergen-Belsen displaced persons camp, which remained open until September 1950.

Lasker's testimony at Luneburg helped seal the fate of several of the guards and staff of Auschwitz and Belsen.

They moved to England in 1946 to join their elder sister Marianne, who had managed to flee Germany in 1941. Anita married Hans Peter Wallfisch, a concert pianist, and together they had two children, a son, Raphael, and a daughter, Maya.

As of 1 January 2019, Anita was still alive at the age of 93. She has played cello and travelled all over the world both as a soloist and as a member of the English Chamber Orchestra. She has also spoken much of her life about her wartime experiences, both from the perspective of a victim and as a witness of Nazism.

Karl Franz Gebhardt

Doctor Karl Franz Gebhardt was a doctor who had worked as the Medical Superintendent at the Hohenlychen Sanatorium in Lychen, north of Berlin. It had first opened in 1902 for the treatment of children with tuberculosis, but by the 1930s it had become one of the main medical facilities of the SS, where both injured and convalescent SS men were treated.

During the Second World War, Gebhardt was the consulting surgeon of the Waffen-SS, the chief surgeon in staff of the SS and Police, and was the personal physician to Heinrich Himmler.

He was also the main co-ordinator of a series of experiments performed on concentration camp inmates at Ravensbrück and Auschwitz. These experiments were an attempt to defend his approach to the surgical management of contaminated traumatic wounds, rather than use the then new innovation of antibiotic treatment of battlefield injuries.

He was arrested after the war and tried at the Nuremberg Doctors' American Military Tribunal No.1 in 1946/7, along with twenty-two other doctors. He was sentenced to death on 20 August 1947, and hanged on 2 June 1948.

Himmler instructed Gebhardt to go to Prague on 27 May 1942 to treat Heydrich, who had been wounded by an anti-tank grenade in an assassination attempt. After surgery, Heydrich became feverish. Hitler's personal physician Theodor Morell, who was also in attendance, suggested to Gebhardt that it might be useful to treat Heydrich with sulphonamide, which was an early form of antibiotic, but Gebhardt declined Morell's suggestion, believing that Heydrich's health would improve without antibiotics. Heydrich died of sepsis on 4 June 1942, eight days after being wounded. This was bad news for concentration camp inmates, on whom Gebhardt would later conduct medical experiments.

Not satisfied, it would appear, with killing Heydrich, he nearly killed Albert Speer too, and he was only treating him for fatigue and a swollen knee. Speer however, not happy with Gebhardt's methods, had him replaced with Doctor Friedrich Koch.

While working at Ravensbrück, Gebhardt began conducting medical experiments on prisoners without the approval of the camp commandant Fritz Suhren. But Gebhardt won the argument when he received the backing of the SS leadership.

Possibly fearing for his own reputation, as it was he who sent Gebhardt to treat Heydrich, Himmler suggested to Gebhardt that it might be useful for him to conduct experiments proving that sulphonamide was no good in treating gangrene and sepsis. Gebhardt agreed, seeing an opportunity to vindicate his actions in Prague. Some of the experiments he went on to carry out included breaking prisoners legs and then infecting the wounds with different organisms.

His other hare-brained idea was to amputate limbs from prisoners and transplant them onto soldiers who had been wounded fighting on the eastern front.

Chapter 9

Bergen-Belsen

Belsen is another ex-concentration camp I have visited. I recall being driven through a forest with very tall pine trees on either side of the road. It was quiet and peaceful, and hard to believe that I would soon be walking into the remains of a Second World War German concentration camp. The car park reminded me of a roadside stop-off area where you find toilets and some kind of café. There was a small museum, and then a walk through into an area that had previously been the concentration camp.

Bergen-Belsen memorial.

There were none of the original camp buildings left, so it was somewhat difficult to comprehend the dark secrets that were hidden in this now desolate location. Most noticeable were numerous large mounds of soil. I later found out that these were the mass graves that had been dug soon after the camp was liberated by British troops in April 1945. There were so many dead bodies lying about that the decision was taken to bury them as quickly as possible to prevent disease.

As I walked around the camp, the only noise I could hear was the distant sound of artillery fire from British troops in training, and there was an eerie breeze gently blowing through the middle of the camp. This was 1985, the cold war was still on, and the Berlin wall was still standing.

In 1935, two years into Nazi Party rule, the Wehrmacht began building a massive military complex, which is still in use today as a training area for NATO military personnel. The camp took just over four years to build, and the men who had carried out the work, many of whom were not local, needed somewhere to live. So the infamous Belsen concentration camp began life as Bergen-Belsen Army Construction Camp. Once the military complex had been completed, the workforce was no longer needed, the men moved out and their homes fell into disrepair. But it wasn't out of action for long. September 1939 saw Hitler invade Poland, and the camp's derelict huts suddenly became needed to house captured Polish soldiers.

In June 1940 the Polish prisoners were joined by Belgian and French prisoners of war.

Germany began planning her invasion of Russia in 1941, and with this in mind, Bergen-Belsen was greatly increased in size and became known as Stalag Xl-C, with a capacity to hold 20,000 prisoners. There were two other camps in the area intended for the same use. The comfort of Russian prisoners of war was not something that Nazi Germany cared much about, and consequently by March 1942, more than 41,000 Russian prisoners of war had died in these camps from exhaustion, starvation or disease and a total lack of any medical assistance.

It was in April 1943 that an area of the Bergen-Belsen camp became transformed into the infamous Belsen concentration camp, when it was taken over by the SS *Wirtschafts-Verwaltungshauptamt,* or the WVHA, the Head Office of Economic Administration. This was where things started to become clandestine about the camp's real purpose. The Geneva Conventions, to which Germany was a signatory, allowed for the international inspection of civilian internment camps, so in June 1943 the concentration camp part of Bergen-Belsen was redesignated as an *Aufenthaltslager*, a holding camp. This was not covered by the Geneva Conventions, which meant that there was no requirement to make it available for international inspection.

Much thought had obviously gone into Belsen and what was going to go on there. Jewish men, women and children were sent there supposedly with the intention of either exchanging them for interned German civilians being held in other countries, or for money. The Germans were quite happy with the premise that if other countries or organisations wanted Jews that badly, then they could pay for them. To make it easier for such a transfer or transaction to take place, the Jews in Belsen were kept in separate, smaller camps. For example, the 'Star camp' was for Dutch Jews, the 'Hungarian camp' was for Hungarians, and the 'Neutrals camp' for Jews from neutral countries. Despite this elaborate planning, only about 2,500 Jewish prisoners were released from Belsen for transporting to other countries. The longer the war went on, such transfers had less chance of happening.

The Nazis even designated part of the camp as the *Erholungslager*, the 'recovery camp', where prisoners from other camps were sent because they were either too frail or sick to work, and once they had recovered sufficiently they would be returned to the work camp they had come from. Or at least that's what they were told. For many the reality was death.

Between 1941 and its liberation in April 1945, it is estimated that somewhere in the region of 50,000 Jewish inmates perished at Belsen. One of the worst periods for loss of life came in the months immediately before the liberation, and those just after. The deaths came about due to a number of factors, none of which were related to the use of gas chambers. Food for the prisoners had become almost non-existent, as was medicine, and sanitation was in an extremely poor state of repair. A combination of these factors caused a continual outbreak of numerous diseases: dysentery, tuberculosis, typhoid fever, and typhus.

Josef Kramer

Josef Kramer had been commandant of Auschwitz II-Birkenau between 8 May and 25 November 1944, and from December 1944 to 15 April 1945 he undertook the same role at Belsen. Such was his penchant for brutality, he earned himself the nickname 'Beast of Belsen'.

Kramer began his concentration camp career in April 1941, when at the relatively young age of 35 he was made commandant of Natsweiler-Struthof, which had a capacity of 1,500 prisoners. It was the only camp in what is today part of France. This was where Kramer's brutal reign began. While at the camp he personally killed eighty out of a group of eighty-six Jews; fifty-seven men and twenty-nine women. Their deaths occurred at the camp's improvised gassing facility, which suggests that it might not have been a hard standing facility, but a mobile unit such as a vehicle into which carbon monoxide gas was pumped. They were killed to become anatomical specimens at the Reich University of Strasbourg, as part of a proposed Jewish skeleton collection under the control of August Hirt. After they arrived on 30 July 1943 they, unlike most other inmates at the camp, were well fed. This was because, apparently, it was intended to make a body cast of each of the corpses before they were literally stripped to the bone. When they had been well enough fed, Kramer then gassed them in four groups on 11, 13, 17, 19, August 1943.

In September 1944, when Himmler knew the war was lost, he ordered that the project be abandoned and all evidence of the Jewish skeleton project destroyed. Unfortunately for the Nazis, but fortunately for the Allies, the order never got through, and when the Allies liberated Strasbourg, they found eighty-six bodies that had been preserved in formalin. This at least allowed for each of the eighty-six to receive a proper burial. Initially they were interred in Strasbourg's Municipal Cemetery, but in 1951 they were transferred to the Jewish Cemetery of Strasbourg-Cronenbourg. The names of the eighty-six appear in the book by Hans-Joachim Lang entitled *The Names of the Numbers* (2004).

August Hirt, who was a captain (Hauptsturmführer) in the SS, had also apparently worked out that he was going to be on the losing side. He didn't even wait until the end of the war before making good his escape. Instead he fled from Strasbourg in September 1944, never to be seen again. He had actually taken himself to Tübingen in southern Germany. He was tried in his absence at the Military War Crimes Trials at Metz on 23 December 1953, where he was found guilty and sentenced to death. Unbeknown to the court, Hirt had committed suicide on 2 June 1945 in the Black Forest.

Kramer moved to Auschwitz II-Birkenau on 8 May 1942 where he became the *Lagerführer*. He remained there until 25 November 1944. He wasn't an armchair commandant who locked himself away in his office, quite the opposite in fact. At his trial, witnesses gave evidence that he had taken an active part in the selection of victims for execution. Not only was he disliked and feared by the inmates of Auschwitz, but also by those who served under him. A Doctor Franz

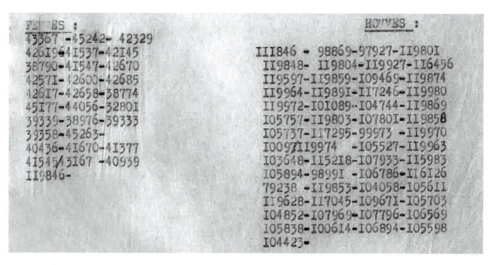

The numbers of the eighty-six victims of Natsweiler-Struthof.

Lucas, who worked at Auschwitz and was sentenced on 20 August 1965 to three years, three months imprisonment for his involvement in the holocaust, gave evidence at the first Auschwitz trial held in Frankfurt. When Lucas saw his name on a list of selecting physicians for a large group of Hungarian Jews, he strongly objected. Kramer's response was, 'I know you are being investigated for favouring prisoners. I am now ordering you to go to the ramp, and if you fail to obey an order, I shall have you arrested on the spot.'

Kramer was transferred to Bergen-Belsen to become commandant in December 1944, which meant that his stay there was just four months long.

At Belsen, the administration of the camp had come to a grinding halt, but despite this, Kramer carried on as if everything was as it should be. By 1 March 1945, the camp contained 42,000 prisoners, and they were dying at the rate of 250 per day, mostly from typhus. Kramer was apparently under the misapprehension that all was well with the Nazi world, and was still writing reports requesting help and resources. None of either were sent, but what he did get was more prisoners, 28,000 of them, who arrived just two days before the camp was liberated.

Belsen was liberated on 15 April 1945 by elements of the British 11th Armoured Division, who had been held in reserve until 28 March 1945. The camp was not something the British troops had been expecting to discover, and when they did, it came as a massive shock. They found about 60,000 starving and sick people in the camp, and didn't have a clue who they were or what they were doing there in the middle of a forest. All were dirty with their clothes, most of which were no more than rags, hanging off of their frail and broken bodies. More shocking still was the discovery of more than 13,000 dead bodies just lying around the camp unburied.

Remarkable as it might sound, Kramer made no attempt to escape, and he was arrested after a cease-fire agreement had been negotiated with the German Army so that the British could take control of the camp. Most of the rest of the camp staff, fearing the worst, had made good their escapes the day before. When the British arrived, Kramer even calmly showed British senior officers around the camp.

A British Army bulldozer pushed bodies into a mass grave following the liberation of Bergen-Belsen, April 1945.

After the British had carried out their enquiries, forty-eight members of the Belsen staff, including Kramer, were arrested. This number included twelve 'Kapos', these were inmates who were trusted by the guards to supervise those they were imprisoned with. The new prisoners at Belsen were ordered to collect up the rotting corpses and bury them.

At the end of the war, Belsen was the only concentration camp which came under the control of the British Army. This meant that captured war criminals who had worked at other concentration camps did not come under British jurisdiction.

On 17 September 1945, Kramer appeared before the British Military Tribunal at Luneberg. Along with Kramer, forty-three out of the forty-eight who had worked at Belsen in some capacity were also tried. Thirty were found guilty.

A mass grave at Bergen-Belsen.

Kramer was found guilty, sentenced to death, and hanged at Hamelin prison on 13 December 1945 by the famous English executioner Albert Pierrepoint. Pierrepoint carried out some 200 executions of people who had been convicted of war crimes.

Irma Grese

There were two other notorious members of staff at Bergen-Belsen who, for different reasons, drew much global attention: Irma Grese and Fritz Klein. Both Grese and Klein were found guilty of the charges against them and sentenced to death by hanging. Their sentences were carried out on the same day as Kramer's at Hamelin prison.

What is staggering in Irma Grese's case is her age: she was only just 22.

Irma Grese was a female guard at Bergen-Belsen.

She was born on 7 October 1923 in Mecklenburg-Strelitz, which had only come into being as a state of the Weimar Republic in 1918 during the German Revolution, which took place in two stages between 29 October 1918 and 11 August 1919. The revolution saw the abdication of Emperor Wilhelm ll and the end of the monarchy in Germany.

Irma was the third of five children born to Alfred and Berta Grese, having two sisters and two brothers. Alfred worked on a farm as a diary worker. The Greses appeared to be a normal happy German family, but in 1936 Berta found out that her husband Albert wasn't as devoted to her as she thought he was, due to him having an affair with a local publican's daughter. Berta was so upset that she committed suicide by drinking hydrochloric acid. Irma was 13 at the time.

She left school two years later and initially went to work at the dairy factory in Fürstenberg, before leaving there later in the year to work in a shop in the nearby town of Lychen, whose claim to fame was that drawing pins were invented there in 1903.

In 1939 her father remarried, but not the woman with whom he had been having an affair. His new wife was a widow with four children. All of a sudden the Grese household had plenty more mouths to feed. Irma then went to work as an assistant nurse at the Hohenlychen Sanatorium, which was also the place of work of the sinister Doctor Gebhardt. She worked there for the next two years, and didn't want to leave, but after failing her apprenticeship, she had to move on.

It is not clear exactly when, or why, but Grese became smitten with both the Hitler Youth and the female wing, the League of German Girls – for girls aged between 14 and 18. There was also the Young Girls League, for girls aged 10 to 14. A third section was added, for girls aged 17 to 21 years of age, called the Faith and Beauty Society. She became obsessed with the Nazi cause.

At the age of 17, Grese enlisted in the 'Female SS Helpers', the training centre of which was near Ravensbrück, a concentration camp for women only, and after she completed her training she volunteered to work at the camp. She hadn't been at Ravensbrück long when she was moved to Auschwitz II-Birkenau as a guard, but moved back to Ravensbrück in around June 1942. In March 1943 she once again found herself back at Auschwitz II-Birkenau, where she worked as a telephone orderly and was a supervisor of various *Kommandos*. In December she became the mail censor.

She obviously excelled at her work, or was well liked by her bosses, because in the latter part of 1944 she was promoted to the rank of *Rapportführerin*, the second highest rank of camp guard. By now her brutality had earned her a reputation and she been given the nickname 'the Beautiful Beast'.

She thought nothing off setting her attack-trained German Shepherd on the camp's prisoners, kicking and punching them, or striking them with the plaited whip that she was hardly ever without. The prisoners didn't have to do anything to be on the receiving end of her pointless brutality; mostly she did what she did for no other reason than that she could. Her sadistic nature had sexual overtones to it. One of her warped party pieces, according to Gisella Perl, a Romanian Jewish gynaecologist and one of the inmates at Auschwitz from 1944, was to whip big-busted women across their bare breasts, and that she appeared to be sexually aroused by their suffering.

Olga Lengyel, a Hungarian Jewish prisoner at Auschwitz II-Birkenau, who survived the Holocaust and later wrote of her wartime experiences in a book entitled *Five Chimneys*, claimed that Grese had an insatiable sexual appetite and that she had affairs with camp guards as casual sexual liaisons whenever she felt the need. Lengyel claims that one of her lovers was Josef Mengele. There were also rumours that she had sex with some of the inmates. When she became pregnant, she had a male Hungarian prisoner who had been a doctor give her an abortion.

At Auschwitz II-Birkenau, Grese was involved with prisoner examination and selection. This macabre task was in the main was carried out and overseen by German doctors wearing SS officer uniforms. As trains arrived from all corners of Europe, they held the lives of the people on these trains in their hands. It was the doctors who would decide who would live and who would die. The criterion was quite straightforward: anybody thought strong enough to undertake slave labour for a prolonged period of time lived, the others were sent straight to the gas chambers, under the pretence that they were having a shower to cleanse them and remove lice.

Grese was a jealous personality. If Mengele selected a fit and attractive woman, Grese would suggest that she had a flaw that made her unsuitable. The truth was more likely that she was prettier than Grese. For some women, this could be sufficient for them to be sent to the gas chamber.

As the Russians arrived and Auschwitz was evacuated, inmates were sent on to Ravensbrück and Bergen-Belsen. But any relief that inmates might have felt at being moved to another camp was short-lived when they realised that Grese had been moved with them to carry on torturing and brutalising them as she saw fit.

Somewhat surprisingly, Grese was still at Bergen-Belsen when British soldiers marched in to liberate the camp on 15 April 1945. She made no attempt to escape, even though she surely must have known the fate that awaited her when she became a prisoner herself.

Despite her promiscuity, Grese had a boyfriend, Oberscharführer Franz Wolfgang Hatzinger, a Czech by birth, who was 36 years old. He had been chief of construction at Auschwitz I until 18 January 1945, when he was transferred to Bergen-Belsen. It would appear that, like Grese, he remained at Bergen-Belsen when it was liberated on 15 April 1945. He died from typhus eight days later. Maybe it was Hatzinger's illness which kept Grese from trying to escape before the camp was liberated.

Her trial took place in Luneburg in 1945. She was found guilty of all charges and sentenced to death by hanging. The sentence was carried out on Thursday, 13 December 1945 at Hamelin prison by Albert Pierrepoint. He was assisted in his duties by Regimental Sergeant Major Richard Anthony O'Neil of the British Army. The following is a description of the events of Grese's execution as remembered by Albert Pierrepoint:

We climbed the stairs to the cells where the condemned were waiting. A German officer at the door leading to the corridor flung open the door and we filed past the row of faces and into the execution chamber. The officers stood to attention. Brigadier Paton-Walsh [who oversaw the detention and hanging of Nazi war criminals] stood with his wristwatch raised. He gave me the signal, and a sigh of released breath was audible in the chamber. I walked into the corridor. 'Irma Grese,' I called. The German guards quickly closed all grilles on twelve of the inspection holes and opened one door. Irma Grese stepped out. The cell was far too small for me to go inside, and I had to pinion her in the corridor. 'Follow me,' I said in English, and O'Neil repeated the order in German. At 9.34 am she walked into the execution chamber, gazed for a moment at the officials standing round it, then walked on to the centre of the trap, where I had made a chalk mark. She stood on this mark very firmly, and as I placed the white cap over her head, she said in her languid voice, 'Schnell.' The drop crashed down, and the doctor followed me into the pit and pronounced her dead. After twenty minutes the body was taken down and placed in a coffin ready for burial.

Grese was the youngest woman to die as a result of being convicted under British law in the twentieth century.

Fritz Klein

Doctor Fritz Klein was born at Feketehalom in Austria-Hungary, which is now called Codlea and is in central Romania. He studied medicine at the University of Budapest, but his studies were interrupted by the First World War and he had to undertake military service in the Romanian Army, in which he served as a paramedic.

In May 1943, Hitler requested Romanian Fascist leader Marshall Antonescu to release all ethnic Germans who were serving in the Romanian Army. Antonescu acquiesced, and all of those released, including Klein, were drafted into the German Army. Klein was attached to the SS Personnel Head Office and posted to Yugoslavia. Why he wasn't immediately attached to a hospital or other medical unit is unclear, but seven months after becoming a German soldier his medical skills were finally used, when on 15 December 1943 he was sent to work at Auschwitz II-Birkenau concentration camp as a doctor in the women's camp. He was also attached to the Gypsy camp, and as one of the camp's doctors, he had to take his turn on the train ramp and be involved in selections.

A year after arriving at Auschwitz he was transferred to the Neuengamme concentration camp. His stay at Neuengamme was short and he was transferred to Bergen-Belsen in January 1945. Like the camp commandant, Josef Kramer, Klein made no attempt to escape when the camp was liberated, in fact he assisted Kramer in showing the British around the camp and handing it over to them.

Doctor Fritz Klein was hanged for his role in the atrocities at Bergen-Belsen.

Klein was famously photographed standing in a mass grave of hundreds of dead bodies at Belsen. The photograph was taken by a soldier of Unit No. 5 of the British Army Film and Photograph Section sometime after 15 April 1945.

Klein was one of the forty-four members of staff from Bergen-Belsen who stood trial at Luneburg between September and December 1945. During the trial, cellist of the Auschwitz Women's Orchestra Anita Lasker, then 20, gave evidence against Klein, Josef Kramer, and the deputy commandant Frank Hössler. All three were found guilty of war crimes and were hanged at Hamelin Prison by Albert Pierrepoint.

When asked how he reconciled his actions as a Nazi with his ethical obligations as a doctor, Klein's answer was:

My Hippocratic oath tells me to cut a gangrenous appendix out of the human body. The Jews are the gangrenous appendix of mankind. That's why I cut them out.

Chapter 10

Neuengamme

Neuengamme concentration camp, near Hamburg, had more than eighty-five sub-camps, which, throughout the course of the war, catered for more than 100,000 prisoners, with twenty-four of the sub camps being for women.

The main Neuengamme camp was established by the SS on 13 December 1938, and was originally a sub-camp to the Sachsenhausen concentration camp at Oranienburg. The SS sent one hundred inmates from Sachsenhausen to help with building work at the Neuengamme camp to increase its size and help operate the brickworks which had also been established there.

It wasn't until 4 June 1940 that Neuengamme was deemed by the SS authorities as being suitable to be classified as an independent concentration camp, and transports then start arriving from all over Germany.

By the time Fritz Klein arrived there in December 1944, the camp was well established and had its own crematorium.

The Celle Massacre

On 8 April 1945, Ukrainian, Russian, Polish, Dutch and French prisoners, who had been held at the Drutte camp, a sub-camp of Neuengamme, were in train freight cars on their way to the concentration camp at Bergen-Belsen. Inmates who had been moved from some of the other sub-camps to the same destination had met at Celle train yards, next to an ammunition train, to continue the journey. In total there were some 4,000 men and women crammed into the train carriages. While they were waiting there, the yards and trains were attacked by the British RAF. The ammunition train was hit by one of the bombs and exploded, resulting in the loss of many of the freight cars which were crammed with inmates from the sub-camps. Those who were not killed in the blast escaped, taking their chance for freedom. Some ran into the town of Celle while others made their way towards the nearby woods. Unfortunately for the escaping prisoners, many of the local residents were Nazis who were only too happy to help the SS troops, Gestapo members, and the local fire brigade hunt them down, and as soon as the air raid finished, the chase began. It is estimated that 200-300 of what history often refers to as the 'hare hunt' victims, were shot and killed as they tried to escape. Another thirty were captured and executed, supposedly for looting in the town of Celle. Now that the train had been lost, the survivors were made to march the rest of the way to Bergen-Belsen. Two days later, on 10 April 1945, the remaining 487 finally finished their journey.

Celle was liberated by the British Army on 12 April who, along with Canadian forces, also liberated Bergen-Belsen three days later.

In December 1947 the Celle Massacre Trial took place. Fourteen people went on trial for the events of 8 April 1945 at Celle; police, military and civilian. Seven were acquitted because of a lack of evidence. Another four were found guilty and sentenced to between four and ten years imprisonment, while the remaining three were sentenced to death. One of the murder convictions was overturned on appeal, and the British military governor showed clemency in the other two cases and commuted their death sentences to imprisonment for 15-20 years. All were released by 1952 for good behaviour.

SS *Cap Arcona*

Orders were given by Gauleiter Karl Kaufmann that the main camp at Neuengamme was to be evacuated of all inmates on 19 April 1945, with the supposed intention that they were to be relocated to a secret new camp, either on the Baltic Island of Fehmarn or the island of Mysen in Norway. By 26 April more than 9,000 prisoners from the camp had been loaded onto four vessels. One of the four was the SS *Cap Arcona* anchored in the Bay of Lübeck. On the evening of

2 May 1945 more prisoners, from the Stutthof and Mittlebau-Dora camps, were loaded into barges and brought out to the *Cap Arcona* and the other vessels waiting there. On reaching the *Cap Arcona* the barge master was told that there was no more room on board, so the barge took them back to the beach at Neustadt. Once there, hundreds were machine-gunned and some beaten to death by their SS guards.

At the Hamburg war crimes trial, the Higher SS and Police Leader of Hamburg, George-Henning Graf von Bassewitz-Behr, told the tribunal that he believed the ships, including the *Cap Arcona*, were to be sunk by either U-boats or the Luftwaffe. Other evidence confirming this was also provided to the tribunal. Simply massacring thousands of men, women and children, by machine gunning them inside one of their own concentration camps wasn't going to look good, so it seems the Nazis came up with a plan to load the *Cap Arcona, Thielbeck,* and *Deutschland* with concentration camp inmates and allow them to be sunk by the Allies. The *Cap Arcona* was not actually seaworthy as her turbines were not in use, and none of the vessels carried any Red Cross hospital markings.

After reaching Lübeck on 2 May 1945, British forces were advised by Mr de Blonay, the representative of the International Committee of the Red Cross, who had an office in the town, that seven to eight thousand prisoners were on board the vessels that were anchored in the Bay of Lübeck. The following afternoon, British forces reached Neustadt where they saw ships on fire in the bay. They rescued some of the survivors, who, despite being emaciated and exhausted, had managed to swim and crawl their way back to the beach. They also found numerous bodies, mainly women and children, who had been massacred by machine-gun fire earlier that day. What the British soldiers didn't know was how the ships they could see in the bay came to be ablaze.

Three ships, *Cap Arcona, Thielbek* and *Deutschland,* were at anchor in the Bay of Lübeck when they were attacked by Typhoon bombers from 184, 193, 198 and 263 Squadrons. They were carrying high explosive rockets, backed up by 20 mm cannon, giving them some formidable firepower. The RAF aircraft were under orders to attack and destroy any enemy vessels they discovered in the Baltic Sea. When they flew over the Bay of Lübeck and spotted the *Cap Arcona, Thielbek* and the *Deutschland,* none of which were displaying Red Cross markings, that is exactly what they did. British commanders believed that a flotilla of ships were being readied in the Bay of Lübeck for escaping senior SS personnel to be transported to German occupied Norway in keeping with Admiral Dönitz's orders that senior SS personnel should be helped to escape Allied capture, even down to issuing them with naval uniforms to conceal their identities.

Out of the approximately 5,000 concentration camp prisoners who were on board the *Cap Arcona*, only 350 survived, while 400 SS men were saved along with 16 of the ship's crew, and 20 SS women. The *Thielbek* saw only 50 out of 2,800 prisoners survive, while all of the 2,000 passengers of the *Deutschland* were saved.

Believing those in the water to be escaping SS personnel, the RAF gunners opened up with everything they had, little knowing that they were killing innocent civilians.

The British and German governments ordered that the records of the incident should be sealed for a hundred years.

Chapter 11

Belzec

The photograph below is of a group of SS officers outside the Belzec extermination camp. L to R: SS Oberscharführer Friedrich Tauscher; SS Unterscharführer Karl Alfred Schluch; unknown; unknown; Action-T4 specialist Karl Gringers; SS Unterscharführer Ernst Zierke; SS Hauptscharführer Lorenz Hackenhalt; SS Oberwachtmeister Arthur Dachsel and SS Rottenführer Heinrich Barbl.

Ernst Zierke
Ernst Zierke was a junior SS section leader who took part in the Nazis' euthanasia programme, more commonly referred to as *Aktion T-4*, an

abbreviation of *Tiergartenstrasse 4*, which was the actual address of the chancellery department responsible for recruitment to Aktion T-4.

It is estimated that 300,000 were murdered during the war in Nazi Germany's euthanasia programme, where patients who were deemed to be 'incurably sick' were given a 'mercy death' or *Gnadentot.*

In the early 1930s Zierke trained and qualified as a nurse and, having been recruited by Aktion T-4 just after the outbreak of the Second World War, he was sent to work at the gassing centres of Grafeneck, Hadamar and Eichberg. The Grafeneck euthanasia centre, at Grafeneck Castle, had become a home for the handicapped in 1929. The Hadamar euthanasia centre was housed in the town's psychiatric hospital.

In 1942, with the snow thick on the ground and the temperatures well below zero, Zierke was sent to the Soviet Union to work as part of the T4's 'Organisation Todt' which was responsible for civil and military engineering programmes. He stayed there for the first three months of 1942, with responsibilities for the forced labour in some of these projects. Zierke then returned to his nursing duties at Eichberg, but three months later he was on the move again, this time to the Belzec extermination camp where his main role was to unload the arriving transport trains of their inhabitants, and then supervise the newly arrived prisoners undressing, before directing them into the gas chambers, which they believed were showers. He left Belzec in March 1943 and went to work at the Dorochuz transit camp at Gmina Trawniki, leaving there in November. Then he was sent to work at the Sobibor extermination camp.

Zierke's last job at Sobibor was to oversee the dismantling of all of its structures, the camp having become non-operational on 14 October 1943. Those actually doing the work were a group of thirty *Arbeitsjuden*, camp inmates whose job it was to load the dead bodies of their fellow inmates into the crematorium. When they had finished dismantling the camp, they were shot dead, often by Zierke.

Zierke finished the war at the Risiera di San Sabba camp complex, and then found himself in a prisoner of war camp where he was arrested, but after being interrogated, he was released. So he went back to his home town where he became a sawmill worker and simply got on with his life. But on 31 January 1963 he was arrested by West German authorities along with a group of other ex-camp guards.

Zierke faced two trials and was acquitted at both. The first was the Belzec Trial which took place at Munich in 1964, the second was the Sobibor Trial at Hagen in in 1965. He died of natural causes in 1973.

Lorenzius Marie Hackenholt

Lorenzius Marie Hackenholt, known as Lorenz, had been a camp guard since the early days of the Second World War and was involved in Operation Reinhard. He began training for the SS on 1 January 1934 and later joined the Death Head troops of the SS. In 1938 he began working at Sachsenhausen concentration camp as a driver mechanic before becoming a guard there. In November 1939 Hackenholt was transferred to Berlin and assigned to Aktion T-4:

> *Photographs of extreme cases of mental illness were shown to us. We were told that the institutions from which the mentally ill were taken were needed as military hospitals. We were further told that gas chambers were to be built in which the victims would be gassed, after which they would be cremated. We had nothing to do with their killing, we would only have to cremate their corpses.*

There were six killing facilities for the mentally ill and Hackenholt worked at them all. His driving skills came in handy as he used to drive SS staff between each of them. For a while he was the driver for a Doctor August Becker, a chemist in the SS whose job it was to deliver bottled carbon monoxide gas to each of the killing facilities.

In 1941 Hackenholt was transferred to what was known as the Lublin Reservation, a complex of concentration camps that had been established in the early days of the war. From there he was sent to Belzec to organise experiments to find a way of killing Jews on a large scale with the use of gas. His first experiment saw him set up three gas chambers in a barrack block that he insulated. Engine exhaust fumes were pumped into them. Using this method he managed to murder more than 50,000 Jews between March and April 1942.

The corpses from these killings were buried in mass graves outside the camp, and when Himmler decided in 1943 that all such evidence of mass killings needed to 'disappear', the mass graves had to be dug up and the bodies burnt. Hackenholt was the man in charge of the operation. After completing his work at Belzec, Hackenholt was sent with some of his colleagues to Trieste, Italy to locate and murder the remaining Italian Jews.

Near the end of the war, Hackenholt was reported to have been killed in Italy. The circumstances of his supposed death were never conclusively confirmed. In 1954 his wife applied to have him legally declared dead as of 31 December 1945, which was agreed by a Berlin court. Despite, the West German authorities decided to investigate. The police even took to conducting surveillance on his wife's home to see if he made contact with her. As part of the investigation, they made contact with Hermann Erich Bauer, a colleague of Hackenholt who was serving life imprisonment at Tegel prison in Berlin for his part in the Holocaust. Bauer claimed with certainty that Hackenholt survived the war, and was living under the assumed name of a dead German soldier, because he had met him near the Bavarian city of Ingolstadt in 1946. Bauer's claims about Hackenholt were corroborated by another man who had been a guard at Sobibor and who had also met Hackenholt in Germany after the war.

Erich Bauer died in prison on 4 February 1980. He had participated in mass executions at Sobibor, some by shooting. He was also in charge of the gas chambers, and known by the prisoners for being vicious and cruel.

Heinrich Barbl

Heinrich Barbl was born in Sarleinsbach in Austria, and before the war had worked as a plumber, fitter, and tinsmith at a nitrogen works in Linz. He joined the Nazi Party in 1938 after the annexation of Austria into Nazi Germany, and was sent to work at both the Hartheim Euthanasia Centre and the one at Grafeneck. His job was to stamp plates with the names of the dead on them, which were attached to urns containing randomly scraped-up ashes. These were then sent out to the families of those who had been killed, who would believe that the urns contained the ashes of their loved ones.

Barbl was posted to Belzec in 1942, where he was often drunk on duty, for which he was punished by being whipped. He was described as not being the brightest of individuals. Camp commandant Gottlieb Hering did not allow him to be involved in the execution of the sick and elderly arrivals at the camp because 'he is so daft that he would shoot us, not the Jews.'

His colleagues were never quite sure if Barbl's drunkenness and apparent stupidity was real, or a pretence so he didn't have to do certain unpleasant tasks.

Barbl ended the war at Sobibor extermination camp where he helped to fit the exhaust piping for the gas chambers.

Remarkably, Barbl was not charged with any war crimes after the war. He was interrogated by Austrian police, but that was as far as it went and he did not appear in any of the post-war trials. Whether that was for of lack of evidence or because it was decided that he had not committed any offences is unclear.

There was no hidden agenda about what happened at Belzec extermination camp: it was where people were sent to be murdered. It was only open for fifteen months – 17 March 1942 until the end of June 1943 – but during that time 500,000 Jews were murdered there, which makes it the third deadliest camp behind Treblinka and Auschwitz.

Undoubtedly many atrocities took place at the Belzec extermination camp, but because there were so few survivors, it has been difficult for historians and governments to build up a picture of the camp's daily mechanism and to establish who was responsible for the crimes which took place there. As far as is known, only seven Jews who performed Sonderkommando duties at the camp survived, and only one of them gave post-war testimony.

Rudolf Reder
Rudolf Reder was born in the Polish city of Debica, and after the war he gave a detailed and moving account of his time at Belzec.

Another man who survived was Chaim Hirszman. But he was shot dead at his home by soldiers of the Tajna Organizacja Wojskowa for joining the new communist militia in a Stalinist Poland. TOW was a clandestine military unit formed before the war in the event of Poland being occupied by a foreign nation.

Reder, who had spent time in the USA before 1919, had started a soap manufacturing business in Lwów, which was successful enough to provide a nice standard of living for him, his wife Feiga and their two children. But their happy family was shattered on 11

August 1942 when they found themselves in one of the first groups of Jews sent from the Lwów ghetto to the Belzec extermination camp. Somebody of his age (he was 61 at the time) would usually have been sent straight to the gas chambers, but the fact that he could speak, read and write German saved him and he was attached to the camp's Sonderkommando. His also worked as a machinist and did maintenance work on the machinery for the gas chambers.

After he had been at Belzec for just over three months, he was part of a prisoner transport to the city to pick up supplies for the camp. The opportunity arose to escape and he took it with both hands, despite knowing that if he was caught, it would mean certain death. He was helped by two women: one a Ukrainian who he knew from before his captivity, and Joanna Borkowska. After the war, Joanna was recognised by Yad Vashem of Jerusalem with the title 'Polish Righteous Among the Nations', an honour awarded to those who helped save Jews during the Holocaust. Reder later married Joanna.

In January 1946, Reder gave evidence before the Commission for Investigation of German Crimes in Krakow, and later that year he published a book, *Belzec*, which, in effect, was the testimony that he had given to the commission. Here is an extract from his book, translated from the Polish:

> *A dozen or so SS men drove the women along with whips and fixed bayonets all the way to the building and from there up three steps to a hall. There the askers counted 750 people for each gas chamber. Those women who tried to resist were bayoneted until the blood was running. Eventually all the women were forced into chambers. I heard the doors being shut; I heard shrieks and cries; I heard desperate calls for help in Polish and Yiddish. I heard the blood-curdling wails of women and the squeals of children, which after a short time became one long, horrifying scream. This went on for fifteen minutes. The engine worked for twenty minutes. Afterwards there was total silence, then the askers pushed open the doors that led outside.*

If it hadn't have been for Rudolf Reder, there would not have been one single first-hand account of this or any of the deaths at Belzec.

In 1949 Reder changed his name to Roman Robak, and in 1950 went to live in the then newly created state of Israel, but in 1953, he and his wife Joanna emigrated to Canada and set up home in Toronto, where he died in 1968.

In 1960 he submitted evidence to the West German authorities for the case against eight ex-SS guards and officers who had worked at Belzec extermination camp during the war. The Belzec trial, held at the First Munich District Court, took seventeen months, 8 August 1963 to 21 January 1965. It was unusual because it was one of the only trials where the defence of having acted under 'superior orders' was accepted as a defence. In both the subsequent Sobibor and Treblinka trials the 'superior orders' defence was not accepted. Accordingly seven of the defendants were acquitted on the grounds that they were acting under duress. Five of these had originally been charged with being an accessory to the collective murders of 360,000 prisoners. One was charged with being an accessory to 170,000 murders, and another for the collective murder of 90,000 murders.

One of the main problems for prosecutors in such cases, and one which was certainly the case at Belzec, was identification by witnesses who couldn't always come up with a name of the person responsible for a crime, describe him, or recognise him, some twenty years after the event. Reder, for one, could not name or describe Josef Oberhauser, or any of the other original defendants, and without confessions it was always going to be a difficult case to prosecute.

Josef Oberhauser was charged with being accessory to a staggering 450,000 counts of collective murder, along with five other crimes of aiding and abetting collective murder in each of 150 cases. For all of those murders he was given the unbelievable sentence of four and a half years and loss citizen's rights for three years. By then the death penalty was no longer an option, but life imprisonment was. Oberhauser had previously been tried and convicted at a court in Magdeburg, in what was then the German Democratic Republic, where he was sentenced to fifteen years imprisonment, of which he served eight.

The seven who were acquitted by claiming the defence of 'superior orders' were Erich Fuchs, Heinrich Gley, Werner Dubois, Karl Schluch, Heinrich Unverhau, Robert Juhrs, and Ernst Zierke.

Chapter 12

Sobibor

Sobibor, along with Treblinka and Belzec, was one of the three extermination camps built by Nazi Germany under Operation Reinhard; their sole purpose was to kill Jews on an industrial scale.

Construction began in March 1942. Its location, in the Lublin district of eastern Poland, was chosen for its isolation and proximity to the railway. It was open for just eighteen months, but estimates of how many Jews were murdered there range from 250,000 to 500,000.

Waiting for the trains to arrive at Sobibor.

The figure suggested by the *Gasmeister* Erich Bauer, in charge of the gas chambers at Lager lll, was 350,000, based on a conversation he had overheard in the camp canteen.

In April 1942, with construction running behind schedule, SS Obersturmführer Franz Stangl took over as commandant, and by the end of the month the camp's gas chambers had been fully installed. To test them, the Nazis brought in 250 Jews from the nearby labour camp at Krychow and gassed them, just to prove that they worked.

Trains full of Jews arrived at Sobibor from all over Europe, day and night, one after another. Once the passengers had disembarked from the cattle trucks they were separated into two lines, one for men, the other for women and children. Depending on the camp's needs at any given time, the guards would be looking for people with certain skills, such as carpenters, blacksmiths, tailors; whatever the particular need was.

There were three sections in the Sobibor camp: Lager I, Lager II and Lager III. Some would be selected and taken off to the hut marked Lager I. Others would be taken to the gas chambers, although the unsuspecting prisoners were told that they first had to have a shower so that they were nice and clean. This was before the use of Zyklon B, and the gas used to kill them at Sobibor was carbon monoxide, produced from an large engine. Those in Lager III had to remove the bodies from the gas chambers, remove any valuables that they might have on them, and dispose of them by either burying them in mass graves or burning them.

The camp started out with three gas chambers, operated from Lager III, and around October 1942 three more were added. This meant that, with each gas chamber being capable of holding 200 prisoners, 1,200 could be murdered at a time.

By about April 1943, not as many Jews were being sent to Sobibor for extermination. This worried the camps Sonderkommando. Their life expectancy was no more than three months at the best of times, because they knew too much about the workings of the camp, what the SS had done, and where the evidence could be found. Now, with less work to do, their prospects looked even bleaker. It was a case of either accept their fate or to try to do something about it. The latter course was decided upon. A committee was formed in secret and various ideas were discussed. They were helped when, on 23 September 1943, a number of Russian-Jewish prisoners of war arrived at the camp from the Minsk ghetto, and the military knowledge they possessed was extremely useful. One of them was Lieutenant Aleksandr 'Sasha' Pechersky, who had been captured by the Germans at Moscow; they discovered he was Jewish, and he ended up at Sobibor. On only his third day at Sobibor, Pechersky did something that could have cost him his life. He stood up to one of the SS senior officers, Karl Frenzel. The following piece is an account given by Leon Feldhendler, who was heavily involved with Pechersky in organising the Sobibor revolt:

Pechersky, still wearing his Soviet Army uniform, was assigned to dig up tree stumps in the North Camp. Frenzel was in charge because an underling was elsewhere and in a bad mood. Frenzel was waiting for an excuse to pick on somebody since he considered himself an officer and a gentleman and waited for some reason to begin his sadistic games. One Dutch Jew was too weak to chop a stump so Frenzel began beating him with his whip. Pechersky stopped chopping and watched the whipping while resting on his axe. Kapo Porzyczki translated when Frenzel asked Pechersky if he didn't like what he saw. Pechersky didn't bow down, shake or cower in fear but answered, 'Yes Oberscharführer.' Frenzel told Pechersky that he had five minutes to split a large tree stump in two. If Pechersky beat the time he would receive a pack of cigarettes, if he lost he would be whipped twenty-five times. Frenzel looked at his watch and said, 'Begin.' Pechersky split the stump in four and a half minutes and Frenzel held out a packet of cigarettes and announced that he always did as he promised. Pechersky replied that he didn't smoke, turned around and got back to chopping down new tree stumps. Frenzel came back twenty minutes later with fresh bread and butter and offered it to Pechersky. Pechersky replied that the rations at the concentration camp were more than adequate and that he wasn't hungry. Frenzel turned around and left, leaving Kapo Porzyczki in charge. That evening, this episode spread through Sobibor. This episode influenced the leadership of the Polish Jews to approach Pechersky about ideas for an escape plan.

Using the darkness of the night, the prisoners' plan was put into action on the evening of 14 October 1943, when the newly formed 'Sobibor underground' sprung in to action, led by Pechersky. The prisoners had the element of surprise as the SS would never have guessed at such audacity.

The plan was to separate the SS officers into two buildings on the premise that new uniforms and boots had arrived for them to try on. Once inside the buildings, the SS men would be killed and their weapons taken. The next step was to raid the camp armoury and set the rest of the camp on fire, and the Ukrainian guards could either surrender or they would be killed. Once all that had been achieved, all six hundred of the Sonderkommando would walk out of the camp's main gates and head for the woods, and then it would be every man or woman for themselves.

The first part of the prisoners' plan went well when they managed to kill twelve of the SS officers. The first to be killed was Unterscharführer Josef Wolf. He was trying on a new coat and they killed him with axes. This same fate befell most of those killed, although it is known that SS Oberscharführer Rudolf Beckmann was stabbed to death in his office.

The dead SS officers were discovered by their colleagues who then fired on the prisoners as they ran for their lives in to the nearby forest. Many were recaptured. It has been estimated that in the actual escape attempt 158 of the prisoners were killed. Another 107 were killed outside the camp by those who had given chase. A further 53 died between the date of the revolt and the end of the war, how is unclear. There were 58 known survivors; 48 men and ten women. Most survivors of Sobibor were those who had escaped during the revolt of 14 October 1943.

After the war, several of the escapees testified at war crimes trials. Moshe Bachir, Jitschak and Ada Lichtman, and Dov Freiberg were witnesses at the Eichmann trial at Yagur in 1961. Josef Duniec died in 1965, the day before he was due to give evidence at the Sobibor trial. Abraham Kohn, who emigrated to Australia after the war, refused to testify against SS Staff Sergeant Karl Frenzel in 1983 as he had never received any compensation for his treatment by the Nazis during the Holocaust.

Thomas Blatt did testify against Frenzel, whose boots he had to clean at Sobibor. Frenzel was sentenced to life imprisonment but was released after sixteen years. Blatt wrote books about his time at Sobibor: *From the Ashes of Sobibor* and *Escape from Sobibor.*

Kurt Ticho Thomas emigrated to the United States after the war and was responsible for initiating trials against two SS men, Hubert Gomerski and Johann Klier, in Frankfurt in 1950. But Klier, who had worked in the Sobibor bakery and shoe-room, had secretly helped the Jews. Some gave evidence on his behalf and he was acquitted on 25 August 1950.

Samuel Lerer arrived at Sobibor in May 1942 where his job was to look after the camp's animals. In 1949 he was instrumental in the arrest of Erich Bauer when he and Esther Terner (née Raab), also a Sobibor escapee, recognised him at a fair in Berlin. He emigrated to America in the early 1950s, where he settled in Brooklyn and became a taxi driver.

Stanislaw Szmajzner was a goldsmith and made jewellery for the SS guards at Sobibor. In 1947 he emigrated to Brazil where in 1978 he was at the São Paolo police station when he recognised deputy commander of Sobibor, Gustav Wagner. Wagner was found dead with a knife in his chest in 1980.

Many of the escapees joined local partisan groups after they escaped.

Leon Feldhendler, one of the main organisers of the revolt of 14 October 1943, fought as a Polish Jewish partisan. He was murdered amid the crime wave of the so-called Soviet liberation.

Ursula Stern joined the local partisans after the escape and in 1945 became the commissioner of a civil militia in Lublin. She later changed her name to Ilona Safran and emigrated to Israel.

Hella Weiss worked as a gardener at Sobibor. Afterwards she joined the partisans and then the Soviet Army and was awarded several medals including the Red Star. After the war she emigrated to Israel.

Alexander Shubayev, who killed deputy camp commandant Johann Niemann with an axe in the escape, joined the Parczew Partisans after the escape and died fighting with them.

Others who joined the Parczew Partisans were Arkady Moishejwicz Wajspapir, who with Jehuda Lerner killed two SS men in the uprising; Catherina Gokkes, who died before the end of the war; Jakob Biskubicz, who later enlisted in the Polish Army; Mordechai Goldfarb; Zyndel Honigman, who had survived a previous escape attempt in November 1942; and Hella Weiss, who later joined the Soviet Army.

Kalmen Wewerik, a carpenter at Sobibor, lost his wife and two children in the Nazi death camps. After escaping Sobibor he also joined the partisans. After the war he married a survivor of Auschwitz, and wrote a memoir about his wartime experiences.

Alexander Pechersky re-joined the Russian Army after he escaped from Sobibor. Rather than being decorated by Stalin, he was sentenced to several months in prison for having laboured while at Sobibor. In January 2016, Pechersky was posthumously awarded the Russian Order of Courage by Vladimir Putin.

Shlomo Podchlebnik arrived at Sobibor in April 1943 with his wife and two children, and discovered that his brother-in-law Chaskiel Menche was also a prisoner there. On 27 July 1943, he and Josef Kopp killed a Ukrainian guard to escape from the camp. After the war Podchlebnik emigrated to the United States where he died in 1973.

Chaim Leist arrived at the Sobibor camp on 23 April 1943. After the war, like Korenfield, he was one of those who emigrated to Brazil, although he eventually moved to Israel where he died in 2005.

Josef Herszman arrived at Sobibor on one of the first transports into the camp and was put to work in the sorting barracks, where the clothes of those who had been gassed were searched through and then placed into neat bundles. After the war he emigrated to Israel.

Some of the escapees lived to great ages. Chaim Engel, who killed Oberscharführer Rudolf Beckmann during the revolt, escaped with Selma Wijnberg and together they survived the rest of the war in hiding. After the war they married. Chaim lived to be 87 and was survived by Selma, who passed away aged 96 on 4 December 2018. Symcha Bialowitz lived to be 101; his younger brother Philip also survived the escape from Sobibor. Aleksej Waisen lived to be 92; Mojzesz Merenstein, 86; Kurt Ticho Thomas, 95; Esther Terner, 92 and Samuel Lerer, 93. The fates of some of the escapees is unknown, but one, Siemion Rozenfeld, is still alive at the time of writing.

The revolt at Sobibor was the largest of its kind during the war, and when Himmler heard of the escape, he ordered the camp to be torn down, including all of the gas chambers, and for the ground to be covered over with asphalt.

Chapter 13

Treblinka

The Treblinka extermination camp took four months to build; work began in April 1942, and it opened on 22 July 1942 as part of Operation Reinhard. Between then and 19 October 1943 when it closed, it has been estimated that 900,000 Jews were killed in Treblinka's gas chambers. Second only to Auschwitz, more Jews were murdered at Treblinka than at any other Nazi death camp.

The camp was under the control of the SS and the prisoners were looked after by the Trawniki guards, who were collaborators recruited from the ranks of Soviet prisoners of war captured during Operation Barbarossa.

Treblinka had two different sites. Treblinka I was a labour camp. Inmates here were forced to work in a nearby gravel quarry, or in the surrounding woods collecting wood needed for the camps. Treblinka II was an extermination camp, whose sole purpose was to murder Jews. When a transport train arrived at the camp, full of Jewish prisoners, most went straight to the gas chambers, but some, usually the fit younger men, were chosen for the camp's slave labour units, called Sonderkommando. At any one time Treblinka I had a workforce of about 1,000 men, who would have to work between twelve and fourteen hours a day. What they had to do was not pleasant, but being selected for it meant they would live a little longer. Their main role was to drag out the bodies of their fellow Jews who had been murdered in the gas chambers, and bury them in large, specially dug graves, or rather pits. In October 1942, Himmler ordered that all the bodies that had been buried outside the camp should be exhumed and burnt, so as to eradicate any evidence of what had gone on at the camp.

When news first spread throughout the Treblinka II extermination camp in the spring of 1943 that it was soon to be closed down, the surviving prisoners feared they would all be killed. They took the decision to do something about it, rather than simply sit and wait until it was too late and they were all finished off by their SS guards.

A resistance movement in the camp had begun in the early months of 1943. The group was formed by Julian Chorazycki, a former captain in the Polish Army, who was also a qualified surgeon. Other members of the uprising's organising committee were Zelomir Bloch, Marcele Galewski, Leon Haberman, Dr Irena Lewkoska, Rudolf Masaryk, Samuel Rajzman, Chaim Sztajer, and Hershi Sperling.

Initially the date of the uprising had been set for 15 June, but it was postponed under the most unusual of circumstances. A train that arrived at Treblinka II in May 1943 contained a number of those who had fought a sturdy fight against the Germans in the Warsaw ghetto uprising. One of those on board had managed to bring a grenade with him, which had not been discovered, and he detonated it in the camp's undressing area. This sent the Nazis into a bit of a panic. Many prisoners were evacuated to Majdanek concentration camp, the number of new arrivals was drastically reduced, and exhumations was greatly speeded up. The organising committee of the Sonderkommando knew that this meant that it was only a matter of time before they were killed.

The new date chosen for their uprising was Monday, 2 August 1943, a hot summer's day. A Monday was chosen because it was the one day of the week when gassing did not take place at the camp, and many of the Ukrainian guards and some of the SS left the camp to swim at a nearby river.

Quickly and quietly they put their plan into action by taking over the armoury, for which they had acquired a duplicate key. They removed 25 rifles and ammunition, 20 hand grenades, and a number of pistols, but before they could gain control of the rest of the camp, their plan was discovered. They managed to set fire to many of the camp's buildings and blew up a large petrol tank, and then the escaping prisoners turned their attention to main gates, to which they all rushed. For many of them, the gates were as far as they got, as they were killed by machine-gun fire from the guards. About 300 did make it through to a degree of freedom, but many of these did not survive: hunted down by their SS captors they were given no quarter, and simply shot dead wherever they were found. But some did escape, and of them, more than 70 are known to have survived the war.

Two who escaped were Hershl Sperling and Richard Glazar. Both wrote vivid personal memoirs about their experiences, and both ended up taking their own lives, Sperling in Glasgow, 1989, Glazar in Prague in 1997. Their testimonies can be easily found on the internet.

By the time of the uprising, Julian Chorazycki had been dead for some four months, having committed suicide on 19 April 1943, fearing that the plan had been discovered by the Germans and that he would be tortured to tell all that he knew about the escape and who else was involved.

Soon afterwards those prisoners who did not make it out of the camp were ordered to dismantle the camp, knowing they would afterwards be killed. After the prisoners had finished in dismantling the camp huts and other buildings, they were lined up by their SS guards and members of the local police, and executed.

It is hard to believe that the first official war trial specifically in relation to Treblinka didn't begin until 12 October 1964. It took place in Düsseldorf in what was then West Germany. Although there were still thousands of Nazis who had committed war crimes during war openly living in Germany, there just didn't seem to be the will or desire to do anything about them. The Cold War had begun, Germany was split in to two countries, and it appeared that everybody had what they saw as more important things to concern themselves with. Great Britain, France and the United States even wanted Germany to rearm, to defend against the Soviet Union.

The chancellor of Germany from 1949 to 1963, Adenauer, had been against the Nuremberg Trials of 1945-6. In 1949 he also demanded the release of those Nazis, including Rudolph Hess, who were held in Spandau prison in Berlin. On 20 September 1949, he made a speech that was anti-denazification, which was an Allied-led initiative to prevent anybody in either Austria or Germany who had been a member of the Nazi party or the SS from holding a position of power, and to remove those who were in such positions. In the same speech he said that he intended to bring in a new law that gave amnesty to all Nazi war criminals, and that he was also going to apply to 'the High Commissioners for a corresponding amnesty for punishments imposed by allied courts.' His argument was that millions of Germans had supported the Nazis, and therefore to continue with denazification would 'foster a growing and extreme nationalism.' It would also mean that those who had been Nazis, or who had supported the party, would be excluded from German life forever.

In 1950 it came to light that his state secretary, Hans Globke, had played a major part in drafting the 1935 Nuremberg Race Laws as part of Nazi Germany's anti-semitic policy. Despite the furore, Adenauer sent out a strong message, but not necessarily the right one: he kept Globke on as his state secretary, saying that his decision was part of his commitment to reintegration.

In the same year Adenauer, knowing that he was in a strong bargaining position, pressured the Western Allies to release all of the war criminals in their custody, stating that their continued incarceration made West Germany's rearmament impossible. Adenauer got his way and the amnesty came into being on 31 January 1951. The amnesty directly benefitted a staggering 792,176 people.

In 1964, with Adenauer no longer Chancellor, there was a wind of change in the country when it came to war crimes. During 1964 and 1965, eleven former SS concentration camp personnel who had worked at Treblinka were put on trial for war crimes.

Kurt Franz, the camp commandant at Treblinka, was sentenced to life imprisonment, as was Heinrich Matthes, the deputy commandant and chief of the extermination area at Treblinka II. Willi Mentz was known to the prisoners as 'Frankenstein' for shooting newly arrived prisoners in the back of the neck and then pushing them into a deep pit that was on fire. He is said to have killed thousands in this manner. He was also sentenced to life imprisonment but was released in 1978 and died three months later. August Miele also received a life sentence. At his trial he calmly described his own actions at Treblinka as if he were deciding which flowers to have in his back garden:

> *There were always sick and crippled people in the transports. There were also those who had been shot and wounded en route by SS Policemen or Latvians who guarded the transports. These ill, crippled and wounded passengers were brought to the Lazaret by a special group of workers. Inside the Lazaret they placed or lay these people at the edge of the pit. When all the sick and wounded had been brought, it was my job to shoot them. I fired at the nape of the neck with a 9mm pistol. Those shot would fall into the pit. The number of people I shot in this way from each transport varied. Sometimes two or three and sometimes twenty or even more. They included men and women, young and old, and also children.*

Gustav Münzberger, who led unsuspecting victims into the gas chambers, received twelve years, but was released after only half the sentence for good behaviour. He died six years after his release. Franz Suchomel, who was responsible for all looted gold and money, was jailed for seven years and released after four. Otto Stadie was sentenced to six years and was released before completing his sentence due to poor health. Erwin Lambert, who built the gas chambers, received four years but was released straight away due to time already served. Albert Rum, who worked in the gas chambers, received three years. Otto Horn was also charged, but was acquitted and walked free from the court.

After the war, Kurt Franz worked in Germany as a labourer on bridges until 1949. From there he moved to Düsseldorf to work as a cook, which had been his pre-war occupation. He carried on with this work until he was arrested at his home on 2 December 1959. A search of his property found an old photograph album that was full of snaps of the Treblinka extermination camp. It carried the title 'Beautiful Years'.

At the Treblinka trials, Franz stunned the court by denying that he had ever killed a single Jewish prisoner, either personally or by having ever set his dog on a Jew. He claimed to have only beaten a prisoner once. But despite his robust denials he was found guilty of the collective murders of at least 300,000 people. He was sentenced to life imprisonment, released in 1993 for health reasons, and died in 1998.

The prisoners had given Franz the nickname 'Lalke', the Yiddish word for doll, because he had a bit of a baby face, not that any of the prisoners would have ever told him so. Every day he would do his rounds of the camp sitting astride his horse. With him he would have a St Bernard dog, named Barry, who had been trained to take down escaping prisoners by his previous owner, Paul Growth, an SS officer who had worked at Sobibor. Franz seemed to derive great pleasure from setting the dog on unsuspecting prisoners, who would either have to contend with having their backsides or genitals bitten by this enormous dog. Franz would kill just for the fun of it. He had been known to shoot prisoners arriving at the camp, while they were still on the train. A survivor of Treblinka, Oscar Strawczyinski, a Czechoslovakian Jew, wrote the following:

Once Lalka was strolling along the platform with a double barrelled shotgun in his hand and Barry in his wake. He discovered a Jew in front of him, a neighbour of mine from Czechoslovakia by the name of Steiner. Without a second thought, he aimed the gun at the man's buttocks and fired. Steiner fell amidst cries of pain. Lalka laughed. He approached him, commanded him to get up, and pull down his pants, and then glanced at the wound. The Jew was beside himself with pain. His buttocks were oozing blood from the gashes caused by the lead bullets. But Lalka was not satisfied. He waved his hand and said, 'Damn it, the balls haven't been harmed!' He continued his stroll looking for a new victim.

In what became known as the 'Second Treblinka Trial' there was just one defendant: Frank Stangl. Stangl had, uniquely, been commandant of both Sobibor, 28 April to 30 August 1942, and Treblinka, 1 September 1942 to August 1943. While he was in charge at Sobibor, more than 100,000 Jews were murdered. From his time at Treblinka he is quoted as saying:

To tell the truth, one did become used to it. They were cargo. I think it started the day I first saw the Totenlager [extermination area] in Treblinka. I remember Wirth standing there next to the pits full of black and blue corpses. It had nothing to do with humanity, it could not have. It was a mass, a mass of rotting flesh. Wirth said, 'What should we do with this garbage?' I think unconsciously that started me thinking of them as cargo. I rarely saw them as individuals. It was always a huge mass. I sometimes stood on the wall and saw them in the 'tube,' they were naked, packed together, running, being driven with whips.

In 1945 Stangl was detained by the Americans, having not bothered to change his name. He escaped from custody on 30 May 1948 and made his way to Italy with SS Sergeant Gustav Wagner and Austrian Roman Catholic Bishop Alois Hudai, a Nazi sympathiser who helped him escape. He made it to Syria where he was later joined by his wife and family. They continued living there for three years, but in 1951 they moved to Brazil, where he ended up working in a Volkswagen factory in São Paulo. The Austrian authorities did not issue a warrant for Stangl's arrest until 1961, despite knowing of the atrocities he had committed, and despite the fact that he continued to use his own name. But in 1967 he was arrested by the Brazilian police, extradited to West Germany and put on trial for the murder of some 900,000 Jews. He admitted what he had done but argued, 'My conscience is clear. I was doing my duty.' He was found guilty and sentenced to life imprisonment, but died of heart failure in prison on 28 June 1971.

Before the end of the war, Treblinka was completely dismantled, the ground was ploughed over, and a farm house built on the site to hide any trace of what had once gone on there.

Chapter 14

Dachau

Dachau was one of the first concentration camps in Nazi Germany. It was in use from 22 March 1933, soon after Hitler and the Nazis came to power. It was initially intended to hold political prisoners, but those who were held there and the reasons why changed over time. It had originally been a gunpowder and munitions factory dating back to the First World War. The first prisoners at Dachau were used as the labour

A photograph taken in April 1945 showing the main gates to Dachau concentration camp, following its liberation.

force to help enlarge the size of the camp, while others worked at a nearby munitions factory. The camp was also used as a base to train SS guards in the ways of concentration camp life.

The following is the content of the original press release by the Nazis, announcing the opening of the Dachau concentration camp in March 1933:

> *On Wednesday the first concentration camp is to be opened in Dachau with accommodation for 5,000 people. All communists, and where necessary, Reichsbanner and Social Democrat functionaries who endanger state security are to be concentrated here, as in the long run it will not be possible to keep individual functionaries in the state prisons without overburdening these prisons and on the other hand these people cannot be released because attempts have shown that they persist in their efforts to agitate and organise as soon as they are released.*

As with many of the concentration camps, *Arbeit macht frei* was emblazoned across the main gates – 'work will make you free'. This in part allowed the Nazis to pretend these camps were simply re-education camps where the inmates were put to work. In fact, the prisoners would be worked so hard that they would die.

Besides the main camp at Dachau, there were just under 100 sub-camps, which could be found dotted about all over the southern part of Germany. The main Dachau camp had standing cells, in which a prisoner could not sit or lie down. Two days in one of these, and a prisoner could be driven insane. Other punishments, not that a prisoner had to have actually done anything wrong to receive one, included floggings, prisoners having their hands tied behind their backs before being hoisted up in the air, and standing to attention for long periods of time.

During the years the camp was open, more than 200,000 people were held as prisoners in the camp, both Jews and non-Jews. The authorities, i.e. the SS, recorded 31,000 deaths in the camp during the time it was open, but the chances are that there were others who died but for one reason or another their deaths were not recorded.

Prisoners at Dachau.

Communists and homosexuals were sent to Dachau, as were Jehovah's witnesses and gypsies. Anyone who spoke out against the Nazis risked being sent there.

During the years they were in power, the Nazis imprisoned a total of three and a half million German nationals for political reasons.

Of these an estimated 77,000 were sentenced to death by the courts.

After the passing of the Nuremberg Laws in 1935, which made racial discrimination a policy of the government, German Jews were sent to the camp. In the early days of Nazi rule, Jews would be offered the freedom to emigrate overseas, but there was a catch: they had to agree to give up their homes and other property voluntarily to the Reich treasury. They also had to find a country to accept them.

On 9 November 1938, the Nazis attacked Jewish homes, businesses, schools and synagogues in what became known as Kristallnacht. About 100 Jews were killed, and more than 30,000 were arrested for nothing other than being Jewish. Some 10,000 of those detained on Kristallnacht were sent to Dachau concentration camp, although most were later released on the promise that they would leave Germany.

Most of those sent to Dachau were used for slave labour. They were rented out to German businesses for a fee paid to the SS.

The prisoners were heavily guarded to ensure that there were no escape attempts. Guard towers with soldiers with machine guns

Himmler visiting Dachau on 8 May 1936.

watched inmates day and night, despite the fact that due to their meagre diet and exhausting work they had very little energy. Inside the camp there were other measures to deter escape. Ten metres in from the electrified fences was a 'no go zone'. Stepping into this would attract a burst of machine-gun fire from one of the guard towers and almost certain death. Some prisoners who could not take any more committed suicide by stepping into the no go zone, knowing that they would be shot. Guards were known to enjoy throwing a prisoner's hat into the zone and telling him to retrieve it, knowing he would be shot.

Dachau had an infamous doctor: Sigmund Rascher. He began the war being conscripted into the Luftwaffe, where he became a captain in their medical service, before transferring to the SS as a private. He became involved in a relationship with, and later married, Karoline Diehl, a well-known German singer, who knew Himmler. This gave Rascher direct contact with Himmler. After having known Himmler for only one week, he presented him with a paper entitled 'Report on the Development and Solution to Some of the Reichsfuehrer's Assigned Tasks During a Discussion Held on 24 April 1939.'

Rascher had become involved in medical tests to find a cure for cancer involving plant extracts. The deputy leader of the Reich Health Ministry, who was also involved in this research, favoured conducting experiments on rats, but Rascher wanted to conduct them on humans. He wrote a letter to Himmler, not covering up the fact that such experiments would more than likely prove fatal for those who took part in them. Himmler agreed with Rascher, and Dachau was fitted out with the relevant medical equipment.

So-called 'freezing experiments' were also carried out at Dachau, to discover ways of warming pilots who had been shot down or who had crashed into the sea and were suffering from hypothermia. The experiments involved leaving naked men out in the freezing cold, or immersing them in ice-cold water for hours. The 'volunteers' would be observed and then warmed up, usually by immersing them in hot water.

Rascher later became involved in experimenting with a blood clotting agent called Polygal. It was intended for the treatment of wounded German servicemen. To test it he used some of Dachau's prisoners. First, the 'volunteer' was given a Polygal tablet, then either shot or had a limb amputated, without anaesthetic, to see how quickly their blood coagulated.

Still his ideas had not been exhausted, and in late 1943 he informed Himmler that he had found a way of extending a woman's natural child bearing age. He claimed that his own wife had had given birth to their three children after the age of 48. This was a lie: he and his wife did have three children, but they had either been purchased or stolen. In fact, while 'pregnant' with their fourth child, Frau Rascher was arrested while trying to steal a baby. When Himmler received word of this, he was not happy. He had been made to look a fool. For Rascher and his wife there was no trial. They were arrested in April 1944, charged with scientific fraud and financial irregularities. Rascher on his own was also charged with the murder of his former lab assistant Erich Hippke, the Luftwaffe's Chief Medical Officer. It later turned out that many of the ideas Rascher claimed as his own were not his own ideas but Hippke's.

Rascher was sent to Buchenwald concentration camp, where he remained until April 1945, and then, ironically, to Dachau, where, just three days before the camp was liberated, he was executed. There are two versions of his death, one that he was executed by a firing squad, the other is that he was shot through the hatch in his cell door by SS Hauptscharführer Theodor Bongatz on the orders of Himmler. At the Nuremberg trials it was noted by the judges that although Rascher was not on trial, they still found that his experiments were inhumane and criminal.

Erich Hippke, the Luftwaffe's Chief Medical Officer.

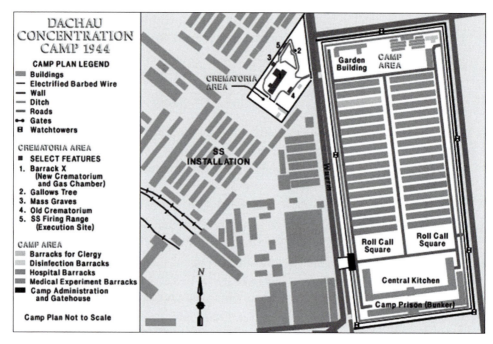

A plan of Dachau concentration camp.

As for Erich Hippke, he was arrested in December 1946, by which time he was working as a general practitioner in Hamburg. He was not charged.

Nazi Germany had had a euthanasia programme since before the war. 'Invalids', both physical and mental, were systematically murdered at Dachau, Jews and non-Jews.

Dachau was liberated on 29 April 1945. At the time there were approximately 65,000 prisoners still there, about 22,000 of whom were Jewish. The dying did not stop. Despite their best efforts, which included two medical units, the 116th and the 127th Evacuation Hospital units, attached to the US 7th Army, treated some 2,252 patients, of which 227 died, from typhus, exhaustion or starvation.

After the war and up until 1948, Dachau was used to house SS prisoners awaiting trial. It was later used as a American military base, and it finally closed in 1960.

Chapter 15

Female Nazi Guards

There were numerous female guards at the concentration camps, some were no doubt quite normal human beings, but many became brutal and murderous individuals, for whom administering beatings and killing became as normal as breathing air.

During the course of the war, some 55,000 guards worked in the concentration camps. Only 3,700 were women, and the only reason that women were ever used in this capacity was because of a shortage of men to do the job.

Execution of Guards and Kapos at Stutthoff concentration camp, 4 July 1946.

It was 1941 when women were first considered for the role of prison guard, and it was 1942 before the first of them arrived at Auschwitz and Majdanek, both in Poland. Their training had taken place at Ravensbrück all-women concentration camp at Furstenberg-Havel in Northern Germany.

They were not used at all of the concentration camps.

They worked at Bolzano in the South Tyrol, a camp for persecuted Jews and political prisoners. After the war the area had a large German population, and even as recently as the 1960s had its own underground secessionist organisation: the South Tyrolean Liberation Committee.

Kaiserwald concentration camp was near Riga in Latvia, built in March 1943. Three large ghettos in Latvia – Riga, Liepaja and Daugavpils – were liquidated of their Jewish inhabitants in June 1943. The few who survived were sent to the Kaiserwald camp. Female guards were there between 1943 and 1944.

From March to May 1945, female guards worked at Mauthausen, one of the first very large camps. There was a camp quarry and

Stutthof concentration camp.

the inmates would have to carry rocks up 186 steps, known to the inmates as the 'Stairway to Death'. Female guards were at the camp between March and May 1945.

Stutthoff was situated near to the Polish town of Sztutowo. Female guards worked at the camp for three years between 1942 and 1945. It was the first concentration camp set up by the Nazis outside Germany, in operation from 2 September 1939. It was initially used for the detention of Polish leaders and intelligentsia, and was the last concentration camp to be liberated by the Allies, on 9 May 1945.

It is estimated that a total of 110,000 people were deported there and that 65,000 prisoners died there. In 1943 a gas chamber and a crematorium were added to the camp, and mobile gas wagons were also brought in.

Doctor Rudolf Spanner worked at Stutthof, and between 1943 and 1944. Sigmund Mazur, who worked at the Danzig Anatomical Institute as a laboratory assistant during the war, confirmed that Spanner had made soap from human fat, which he named Reines Judische Fett – pure Jewish fat. After the war however, Spanner was not put on trial, or even arrested.

An example of a mobile gas wagon.

The largest of the twenty-two concentration camps in Estonia was situated near the railway station in the village of Vaivara. Female guards worked there between 1943 and 1944. It was open between August 1943 and February 1945 and housed some 20,000 Jewish prisoners, most coming from the Jewish ghettos of Vilna and Kovno.

The Germans had a programme for oil and shale extraction in the region and needed workers, or rather slaves. As a result, there were no large-scale killings at Vaivara. Only the old and sick were killed, and young children.

In November 1943 the camp was struck with a typhoid epidemic, which killed some 1,600.

The commandant was Hans Aumeier, who had also previously been deputy commandant at Auschwitz. After the war he was arrested by the Allies and in 1946 he was sent to Poland to stand trial for crimes of mass murder he had committed while at Auschwitz. Despite his denials, he was found guilty and sentenced to death by hanging. The sentence was carried out on 28 January 1948.

Vught is in southern Holland, the name of the concentration and transit camp that it had in its midst was Herzogenbusch, which also had fourteen sub-camps in the surrounding area.

Female guards worked at Herzogenbusch and were known as Female SS Helpers – *Helferin*. There were a staggering eleven supervisory levels within that title: *Chef Oberaufseherin* (senior supervisor), *Lagerführerin, Oberaufseherin, Erfstaufseherin, Rapportführerin, Arbeitsdienstführerin* (work recording leader), *Arbeitseinsatzführerin* (work input leader), *Blockführerin, Kommandoführerin, Aufseherin, Arrestführerin* (arrest supervisor).

On the morning of 26 October 1944, 329 prisoners were lined up just outside the camp and shot by the SS guards. Later that morning, soldiers from the 96th Battery, 5th Anti-tank Regiment, of the Royal Canadian Army, arrived outside the camp and were met by a number of SS guards, not to surrender, but to fight. After the Canadians defeated the SS guards, they entered the camp to find about 600 prisoners who were still alive, and who had apparently been due to be shot that afternoon.

The camp at Vught.

A teenage girl, Helga Deen, stayed at Herzogenbusch for a short period before being sent to Sobibor, where she was murdered on 16 July 1943. She wrote a diary of her time at the Vught camp, which she managed to hand over to her boyfriend, Kees van den Berg, who was also there. The diary didn't come to light until 2004, when the son of van den Berg handed it over to archivists in Tilburg, Holland.

Many of the female guards had relationships with their male counterparts in the camps. At Buchenwald, female supervisor Ilse Koch was the wife of the camp commandant, Karl-Otto Koch. Koch had served as a soldier in the First World War, being awarded the Iron Cross 2nd Class before being captured by the British and spending the rest of the war in a prisoner of war camp. On returning to Germany he managed to secure work as an insurance clerk, and in 1930 ended up being sent to prison for forgery and embezzlement. Soon after being released, he joined the SS.

Koch married Margarete Ilse Kohler on 25 May 1936, and fourteen months later he was put in command of the newly opened concentration camp at Buchenwald, on 1 August 1937, where he remained until September 1941. The Kochs went on to have three children, two daughters and a son.

Ilse began working at the Sachsenhausen concentration camp near Berlin, used primarily for political prisoners, in 1936 as a guard and a secretary. At the time she was engaged to the commandant, Karl Koch, and the pair were married the same year. In 1937 Karl

Karl-Otto Koch was the first Commandant at Buchenwald and Sachsenhausen.

Koch was transferred to Buchenwald as its new commandant, and Ilse went with him.

It wasn't long before rumours began to surface about her acts of cruelty. It was said that she had skinned dead bodies and kept their tattoos.

The couple were separated in 1941 when Karl was sent to set to Majdanek while Ilse stayed at Buchenwald.

In early 1941 SS Obergruppenführer Josias, Prince of Waldeck and Pyrmont, was looking at the lists of those who had been executed at Buchenwald, when he saw the name of Doctor Walter Krämer, who had been a chief hospital orderly at the Buchenwald camp. Josias recognised the name because Krämer had treated him. Taking the matter further he discovered that Koch had Krämer and his assistant Karl Peixof killed as political prisoners. The reason why Koch had been so keen for both to die was they had treated him for syphilis, and he was afraid that they might mention it to someone.

In 1943 Ilse and her husband were charged with embezzlement, but she was acquitted due to the lack of evidence and released. She went to live in Ludwigsburg in Baden-Wurttemberg, until she was arrested by American authorities on 30 June 1945. In 1947, along with thirty other defendants, she appeared before an American military court at Dachau. The charges against her were 'participating in a criminal plan for aiding, abetting and participating in the murder at Buchenwald.' She was sentenced on 19 August 1947 when she was eight months pregnant.

Meanwhile, her husband Karl had been tried, found guilty, sentenced to death, and executed by firing squad on 5 April 1945, so the child could not have been his. Ilse was sentenced to life imprisonment for 'violation of the laws *Ilse Koch.*

and customs of war.' On 8 June 1948, Lucius D. Clay, the interim military governor of the American Zone in Germany, reduced the sentence to four years because 'there was no convincing evidence that Ilse Koch had selected inmates for extermination in order to secure tattooed skins, or that she possessed any article made of human skin.' There was a public outcry about this decision.

Jean Edward Smith, an American biographer and distinguished professor of political science, later wrote a book about Lucius D. Clay. The book included the following passage:

> *There was absolutely no evidence in the trial transcript, other than she was a rather loathsome creature, that would support the death sentence. I suppose I received more abuse for that than for anything else I did in Germany. Some reporter had called her the 'Bitch of Buchenwald', had written that she had lamp shades made of human skin in her house. And that was introduced in court, where it was absolutely proven that the lampshades were made out of goatskin. In addition to that, her crimes were primarily against the German people, they were not war crimes against American or Allied prisoners. Later she was tried by a German court for her crimes and was sentenced to life imprisonment. But they had clear jurisdiction. We did not.*

Ilse was rearrested by West German authorities in 1949 and tried before a West German court in a case which began on 27 November 1950. The prosecution produced 200 witnesses against Koch, while a further fifty were produced in her defence. One of the main charges against her revolved around the lampshades, but the prosecution had to drop the charge.

With the case over and a decision reached that she was guilty, a 111-page document then had to be read out which contained the verdict and the reason behind it. The crux of the matter was that despite the two trials she had faced at the end of the war, she had never been charged with crimes against humanity by Germans and Austrians. She was found guilty and sentenced to life imprisonment and the permanent forfeiture of her civil rights. Despite making numerous appeals to the Federal Court of Justice, the Bavarian Ministry of Justice, and the International Rights Commission, she failed.

One of the two sons she had with Karl Koch committed suicide. Her son conceived in prison was named Uwe. He was born in Aichach women's prison, near Dachau. The child was immediately taken away from Ilse at birth and given out for adoption. When he was 19 he discovered who his real mother was and visited her in prison.

Koch committed suicide in her cell at Aichach women's prison by hanging herself, on 1 September 1967.

In addition to Irma Grese (see p.93), another notorious female guard was Maria Mandel. On 15 October 1938 she joined the staff of the Lichtenburg concentration camp, located in a castle at Prettin, Saxony, as a supervisor. She was one of fifty women who worked at the camp.

The newly opened Ravensbrück concentration camp for women was the next camp she found herself at, when she was transferred there on 15 May 1939. A combination of what is difficult to refer to as 'her hard work', and the fact that she joined the Nazi Party on 1 April 1941, saw her promoted to the rank of Oberaufseherin in April 1942. Her new-found position involved drawing up the daily assignments for the camps *Aufseherinnen*, overseeing the camp's daily roll call, and organising and carrying out any beatings that prisoners had been awarded.

Maria Mandel

Maria Mandel was a female guard at Auschwitz.

After three and a half years at Ravensbrück she was transferred to Auschwitz II-Birkenau, arriving there on 7 October 1942, where she became

Oberaufseherin of the female camp, taking over the roll from Johanna Langefeld.

Mandel's new position gave her considerable power. She could never outrank a male SS guard, but she had absolute power over the female prisoners her subordinates. And it wasn't only Auschwitz ll-Birkenau that she was in charge of. She ran all the Auschwitz female camps and subcamps, which included the ones at Hindenburg in Poland and Lichtewerden and Raisko in Czechoslovakia.

Mandel, it could be said, was responsible for inflicting Irma Grese on the prisoners of the camps she worked at. She took a liking to the young Grese and promoted her to the head of the Hungarian women's camp at Birkenau.

Mandel needed just the smallest of reasons to have a prisoner beaten or even killed: quite often it might be for something as ridiculous as the fact that they had looked at her. She was undoubtedly a sadist. She thought nothing of manipulating the women under her control through fear, and did not hesitate to inflict physical violence on anybody who she chose. Mandel's nickname was *The Beast* and she was responsible for the deaths of an estimated 500,000 women and children mostly by sending them to the gas chambers.

Mandel was awarded the War Merit Cross, 2nd Class for meritorious service to Nazi Germany.

She left Auschwitz in November 1944 and was transferred to the Dachau sub-camp of Muhldorf, a much smaller camp. Had she fallen out with someone of rank and importance? Had she been in a relationship with someone who no longer wanted to be involved with her? Her place at Auschwitz was taken by Elizabeth Volkenrath, who remained there until it was closed.

As the Allies were coming closer, Mandel fled from Mühldorf, into the mountains of southern Bavaria, and to Münzkirchen where she was born. She was eventually arrested by the Americans on 10 August 1945 and held in detention. In November 1946 she was handed over to the Polish Peoples' Republic and a year later was tried in Krakow at the Auschwitz Trial, found guilty, sentenced to death, and hanged on 24 January 1948.

Herta Bothe was a normal girl born into a middle-class working family. Her father owned a shop in their home town of Teterow. Herta worked there for a while after leaving school.

In 1939 she became a member of the League of German Girls, the female wing of the Nazi Party youth movement, for girls between 14 and 18 years of age.

In September 1939, aged only 18, she trained to become an Aufseherin at Ravensbrück, about fifty miles north of Berlin. After successfully completing a four-week course she was sent to work as an overseer at the Stutthof

Herta Bothe. Her brutality earned her the nickname 'the Sadist of Stutthof'.

concentration camp near Danzig, now Gdansk in Poland, where her brutal treatment of camp prisoners earned her the nickname 'the Sadist of Stutthof'.

On 21 January 1945, Bothe was one of a number of camp guards tasked with accompanying a group of women prisoners on a journey from central Poland to Bergen-Belsen in Germany, a distance of 900 kilometres. They arrived at Bergen-Belsen at the end of February 1945 and the camp was liberated by the British less than two months later, on 15 April.

Bothe and many other female guards were at the camp when it was liberated, and made no attempt to escape. She was never going to be hard to identify, as she is reported to have been 6 feet 3 inches tall.

The British forces who liberated Bergen-Belsen forced the camp guards to pick up all of the dead bodies lying around the camp and place them in to a mass grave that had been dug outside the camp's perimeter. The guards were not allowed to wear gloves while doing this, with the risk of typhus, which the British soldiers had no sympathy about. Some of the bodies were so rotten and decayed that as the guards picked them up the arms and legs tore away from the torso. The smell was absolutely horrendous and camp guards were not provided with facemasks. After they had buried all of the bodies, they were arrested and taken to nearby Celle for interrogation.

The Belsen Trial took place at the old gymnasium at Lindenstrasse in Luneburg. It commenced on 17 September 1945, lasted for 54 days, and dealt with some 45 defendants.

Bothe was characterised as a 'ruthless overseer' who showed no care or compassion for the prisoners under her control. Bothe admitted to striking inmates with her hands for minor violations of camp rules, but she was adamant that she never beat anyone with a stick or a rod, and that she never killed anybody. Her testimony was contradicted by two witnesses who had been prisoners at

Gymnasium at Lindenstrasse, Luneburg.

Bergen-Belsen when Bothe worked there. The first told how she had seen her beat a Hungarian Jew named Eva to death with a wooden block, while another said he had witnessed her shoot two prisoners for no apparent reason.

Despite these eye-witness statements, which the court believed, Bothe was only sentenced to ten years imprisonment, and after serving just six she was released on 20 December 1951 by order of the British government.

Some of the other female camp guards detained at Bergen-Belsen were Hildergard Kanbach, Magdalene Kessel, Irene Haschke, Herta Ehlert and Elisabeth Volkenrath.

Elisabeth Volkenrath (née Muhlau) was 26 when she arrived at Bergen-Belsen in February 1945, where she performed the role of Oberaufseherin.

Her concentration camp days began in October 1941 when she volunteered for a job as Aufseherin at Ravensbrück. She remained at Ravensbrück for six months and was transferred to Auschwitz II-Birkenau in March 1942. She contracted typhus, but unfortunately for the prisoners she survived. At Auschwitz in 1943 she met and married SS-Rottenführer Heinz Volkenrath.

She was involved in the selecting of prisoners for the gas chambers, and must have impressed her superiors as in November 1944 she was promoted to Oberaufseherin and placed in charge of all of the female camps at Auschwitz. But her stay there was to be short lived, as in January 1945, with the Russian push towards Poland in full swing, the order was given to evacuated the camp. Elisabeth Volkenrath was one of those who accompanied the prisoners on the long march to Bergen-Belsen, where she remained as Oberaufseherin until the British arrived.

She was charged with war crimes and crimes against humanity, mostly at Auschwitz. She was found guilty and hanged on 13 December 1945 by Pierrepoint.

Hermine Braunsteiner was born in Vienna on 16 July 1919. She wanted to become a nurse, but was not able to pass the exams, so instead she became a maid and worked for an American couple in London between 1937 and 1938, so she could speak good English.

Majdanek concentration camp.

After gaining her German citizenship, she returned home to Austria, but the same year she relocated to Berlin, where she lodged with a policeman and his family, and got a job in the Heinkel aircraft factory. After a suggestion by her landlord, she applied to become a prison guard and on 15 August 1939 she went to Ravensbrück to begin her training under Maria Mandel. Her new job was much better paid.

After completing her training, she remained at Ravensbrück, working as an Aufseherin for the following three years, until 16 October 1942 when she moved to the Alter Flughafen forced labour camp, near Majdanek, Lublin, which had been opened in 1941. The reason for the sudden move was supposedly because Braunsteiner had a falling out with Mandel. Majdanek was both a labour camp and an extermination camp (*Vernichtungslager*) which had gas chambers and a crematorium.

After three months, Braunsteiner was moved, along with most of the other camp guards, to the main Majdanek camp, and in January 1943 she was promoted to assistant wardress under Elsa

Ehrich, who, after the war, would be tried in Lublin, found guilty and sentenced to hang.

Braunsteiner enjoyed her work. She thought nothing of brutalising prisoners or murdering them for no reason. She was infamous for her rages. After the war, camp survivors who gave evidence at her trial described how she would grab hold of children by their hair and swing them through the air before throwing them onto the back of a truck that was heading for the gas chamber. Evidence was also given that she killed prisoners by stomping on them until they were dead. This earned her the nickname of 'The Stomping Mare'.

Like Mandel, Braunsteiner was awarded the War Merit Cross, 2nd Class.

In January 1945, with the war not going the way Nazi Germany would have hoped, Braunsteiner was instructed to return to Ravensbrück. She was made Oberaufseherin at the Ravensbrück sub-camp of Genthin, where she was alleged to have killed at least two people by whipping them to death.

On 7 May 1945, Braunsteiner fled the Genthin camp just before the Russians arrived, and fled to Vienna where she remained at large for a year before being arrested and handed over to the British military forces of occupation. She remained incarcerated until the case against her was heard in Graz. She was found guilty of crimes against humanity and human dignity, and of torture and maltreatment of prisoners under her control, but for some reason this was only in relation to her time at Ravensbrück, and not at Majdanek. Almost unbelievably, she was sentenced to only three years imprisonment, and was released after only two. After her release an Austrian court granted her amnesty from any future prosecution for anything to do with her wartime activities. But that didn't stop other countries asking for her extradition.

Hermine Braunsteiner worked at Ravensbrück and Majdanek camps.

Sometime in the mid-1950s Braunsteiner met an American, Russell Ryan, when he was on holiday in Austria, and in October 1958 they married. They emigrated to Nova Scotia, and then in April 1959 they moved to America where on 19 January 1963, Braunsteiner, or rather Mrs Ryan, became a United States citizen. Mr and Mrs Ryan set up home in the Maspeth district of Queens in New York where they became known as a happy, hardworking couple.

Sometime around the end of 1963, or early 1964, the well-known Nazi hunter Simon Wiesenthal picked up the Braunsteiners' story after having been approached by several Majdanek survivors while eating a meal in a restaurant in Tel Aviv. Wiesenthal made enquiries and managed to trace Braunsteiner to Queens, but that was as far as he could take the matter. He contacted the *New York Times*, who appointed a young and inexperienced reporter named Joseph Lelyveld to the case. He found Braunsteiner living at 52-11 72nd Street, Maspeth. She greeted him at the front door of her home and was happy to talk to the young amiable reporter. She told him she had only worked at Majdanek for a year, eight months of which had been in the hospital.

After a case that went on for some three years, the US authorities revoked Braunsteiner's American citizenship, and she was denationalised in 1971. She and her legal team fought against deportation all the way, but in 1973 she was eventually extradited to Germany after a Düsseldorf prosecutor investigated the part she had played in the Holocaust. On her arrival in Düsseldorf she was arrested and remanded in custody. She argued that the Düsseldorf court did not have jurisdiction over her as she was Austrian and not German, and that the alleged offences had taken place outside Germany. But the court was having none of it, pointing out that at the time of the offences she was a German citizen, as well as being an official employee of the German government.

She remained in custody for nearly two years before the case came to court on 26 November 1975, which has gone down in history as being the longest and most expensive case in West German legal history. She was acquitted of six of the charges against her due to insufficient evidence, but found guilty of three. These included the murder of 80 prisoners under her charge, abetting the murder of 102 children, and collaborating in the murder of a further 1,000 prisoners at Majdanek concentration camp. She had been on trial with fifteen other SS men and women who had worked at the camp.

On 30 June 1981, she was sentenced to life imprisonment and was released from Mulheimer women's prison in 1996, in part because of her poor health which had resulted in her needing one of her legs amputated. She died three years later, aged 79.

Because of this case the US Department of Justice Office of Special Investigations was set up, with the purpose of seeking out those who had committed war crimes in the Second World War and who had subsequently become US citizens.

Jenny Wanda Barkmann worked at the Stutthof SK-II concentration camp as an Aufseherin, where she was sadistic and brutal. She was arrested in May 1945 at a railway station in Gdansk, having fled from Stutthof as the Russians approached. At her trial she displayed some bizarre behaviour. She spent much of the trial giggling, laughing, and playing with her hair, and is said to have flirted with some of her guards. When found guilty she said, 'Life is indeed a pleasure, and pleasures are usually short.' She was publicly executed, aged 24, on 4 July 1946, along with ten other female guards from Stutthof, by hanging at Biskupia Gorka Hill, Gdansk.

Another was Ewa Paradies, who was 25 at the time of her hanging at Biskupia Gorka Hill. One witness said of her at the trial: 'She ordered a group of female prisoners to undress in the freezing cold of winter, and then doused them all with ice cold water. When the women moved, Paradies beat them.'

Chapter 16

When Did the Allies Know?

In March 1942, Himmler paid a visit to the Polish government where he presented them with an order for the extermination of 50 per cent of Polish Jews by the end of the year – this was reported to Allied governments.

The Polish Ministry of Foreign Affairs sent a report to the governments of the United Nations, dated 10 December 1942. It was given the unambiguous title of 'The Mass Extermination of Jews in German Occupied Poland'. It pointed out that during the course of the previous three years, the Polish government had lodged a number of protests with mainly Allied nations of the world condemning Germany for her repeated violations of international law and of the basic principles of morality since the invasion on 1 September 1939. The report further noted that despite warnings and declarations by President Roosevelt, Winston Churchill, and Molotov, the

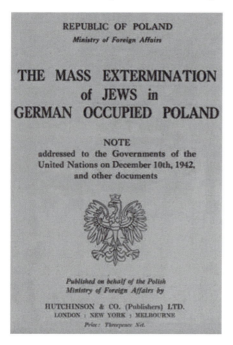

The front cover of the Polish Government's report.

Russian foreign minister, Nazi Germany had not ceased in applying its methods of violence, terror and murders.

In a similar report, dated 3 May 1941, the Polish government provided the Allied and Neutral powers with a comprehensive list of all acts of violence perpetrated by German forces against the population of Poland, based on religious or cultural heritage, as well as the numerous acts of damage and destruction to homes and other buildings across the country. After the report, these acts of violence, far from stopping, only increased in number and level of brutality. As the months went by, these acts were particularly directed against the Jewish population, who were subjected to a system calculated to bring about their complete annihilation as a race. Germany's actions were in also keeping with the public statements that the Nazi leadership were making. The Polish government wanted to bring these facts to the attention of all right-minded people of the civilised world.

By the time of the first report, the Polish government had already, on several occasions, drawn to the attention of the Allied nations to the conduct of the German government. It was made blatantly clear that the methods being used were 'to reduce the population to virtual slavery and ultimately to exterminate the Polish nation.' The report also pointed out that the Germans were pursuing the same policies in other countries as well.

At a conference held at St James's Palace in London on 13 January 1942, the governments of the occupied nations placed among their principal war aims the punishment through the organised justice of individuals responsible for war crimes, whether they ordered them, committed them, or participated in them.

As German troops fought their way into more countries, the number of Jews under German control greatly increased. The reports of murders reached such proportions that people refused to believe them, even when confirmed by the most reliable of witnesses. In Wilno more than 50,000 Jews were reported to have been massacred; in Lwów the figure was 40,000; in Rowne 14,000; and in Kowel 10,000.

Initial reports of these murders spoke of shooting, but there were subsequent reports of new methods such as poison gas. In Belzec it was reported that the Germans had built a camp where they could carry out the murder of Jews by electrocution.

The report of 10 December 1942 talks of deportees arriving at Belzec, Sobibor, and Treblinka 'being stripped and killed by various means, including poison gas and electrocution. The dead were interred in mass graves dug by machinery.' It reported that Belzec, Sobibor and Treblinka had, by 1942, stationary gas chambers which used carbon monoxide gas that was generated by using diesel engines. Concerning the disposal of the bodies, Crematorium 1 at Auschwitz was in operation from 15 August 1940.

Point 15 of the report states:

According to all available information, of the 250,000 Jews deported from Warsaw ghetto up to September 1ˢᵗ, 1942, only two small transports, numbering about 4,000 people, are known to have been sent eastwards in the direction of Brest-Litovsk and Malachowicze, allegedly to be employed on work behind the front line. It has not been possible to ascertain whether any of the Jews deported from the Warsaw ghetto still survive, and it must be feared that they have all been put to death.

On 17 December 1942, Count E. Racznski, Polish Acting Minister of Foreign Affairs, made a radio broadcast. He said that for three years, Germany had done everything that she could to hide from the eyes of the world the martyrdom of the Polish nation, the likes of which had never been seen before in the history of mankind. He added that the Polish government saw it as their duty to inform all interested governments of these events and to draw to their attention the depth of the horror of the situation. It was, he said, Germany's intention to enslave the people of his county before ultimately exterminating the entire Polish nation.

The problem for the Allied nations was: What could they do about it? Concentration camps were in many different parts of Europe, all in areas under German military control. It would have been difficult, if not impossible, to locate these camps, get a sufficient number of troops to them, overcome the guards, and bring the inmates to safety.

The report estimated that up to that date, about 130,000 Polish Jews had been murdered, and it appealed to other nations to 'condemn the crimes of Nazi Germany, punish those responsible and devise a means of offering hope that Germany might be effectively restrained from continuing to apply her methods of mass destruction.'

It would appear that the British government took the Polish report seriously, as also on 17 December 1942, Foreign Secretary Anthony Eden announced in the House of Commons, 'The German authorities are now carrying into effect Hitler's often repeated intention to exterminate the Jewish people of Europe.'

Chapter 17

Newspaper Articles

A 23-year-old German refugee, Fritz Sommerfield, was living in England at the beginning of the war, worrying about his brother and sister who were being held in a concentration camp in Nazi Germany. Since he had been in England, he had received news that his mother had committed suicide in Germany. On 22 May 1939, Fritz himself was found dead, hanging by his belt in the wardrobe at a friend's flat in Fitzjohn's Avenue, Hampstead. A curious fact was that Mr Sommerfield, at over 6 feet tall, was taller than the wardrobe he was found in. It was believed the loss of his mother and the incarceration of his two siblings had affected him deeply. At the time, although the existence of concentration camps in Germany was known about, the fact that people were being brutalised and murdered in them wasn't.

In the second half of 1939 there was much talk in British newspapers of concentration camps in Germany, but it was thought their main use was for dissidents or agitators. The Nazis had been unable to completely keep the concentration camps a secret, as news of their existence and what went on in them had inevitably leaked out.

A group of 500 fugitives had made their way to England and been put up in an old First World War army camp, called the Kitchener camp, situated at Richborough near Sandwich. There were doctors, scientists, lawyers, architects, clerks, brick-layers, plumbers, locksmiths and carpenters, and many were Jewish. The plan wasn't for them to remain in England, but to send them to America and other English speaking countries.

Dr Hanfstaengl was the son of a Munich family of high repute, and one of his godfathers was the Duke of Saxe-Coburg-Gotha, brother-in-law to Queen Victoria.

He had worked for the Nazi Party and been a personal friend of Adolf Hitler. His story came to light as a result of a libel action heard in the King's Bench Division in London on 18 May 1939. The plaintiff was Dr Ernst Hanfstaengl, a doctor of historical literature. The defendants were Selfridge and Co Ltd, who had sold the American journal *New Republic*. Dr Hantstaengel was described in the 27 April 1938 edition of the journal as being 'famous as Hitler's boyfriend until he became the victim of a Palace intrigue.'

Dr Hanfstaengl had given shelter to Hitler after the unsuccessful Munich Beer Hall Putsch of 1923, an attempt by Hitler and his followers to seize power when 2,000 Nazis marched to the Feldherrnhalle. In the ensuing stand-off, sixteen Nazis and four police officers were killed. Hitler was wounded, but escaped arrest only because he was taken to the safety of Dr Hanfstaengl's home. Two days later Hitler was arrested and charged with treason.

Hanfstaengl first met Hitler in 1922 when the Nazi Party, led by Hitler, was a small and insignificant opposition party. It was in 1931 when he accepted a position in the Nazi Party, as what he himself described as a liaison officer between the Nazis and the foreign press. He did not agree with concentration camps and the party's policy towards religion – a reference to Judaism. Disillusioned with where the party was going, he left Germany in 1937 for England to start a new life there.

Dr Hanfstaengl had fallen out with Hitler in the early 1930s when he had several disagreements with Minister of Propaganda, Josef Goebbels. Matters worsened and in 1933 he was removed from Hitler's staff. Giving evidence, Dr Hanfstaengl said that his friendship with Hitler had ended in 1934 and since that time the two had not spoken. In 1936 he was denounced by the British socialite Unity Mitford, who was an ardent devotee of Hitler and anti-Semitic.

In 1937, during the Spanish Civil War, Hanfstaengl received orders from the German government to go to nationalist Spain to assist in negotiations. This involved him being flown to Spain and parachuting to his pick-up point. During the flight, Hanfstaengl became anxious and questioned the pilot, who admitted he had been ordered to drop him not in a nationalist area, but over a republican held area, where, if captured, would have meant certain death. Somehow Hanfstaengl managed to convince the pilot not to do as he had been ordered. Instead they landed at Leipzig Airport and the pilot claimed he had an engine malfunction. Feeling unsafe in Germany, Hanfstaengl escaped via Switzerland to England. Hanfstaengl later said that he believed he was to be thrown out of the aircraft somewhere over Germany, either without a parachute, or, if with one, one that didn't work. Such were the dangers of disagreement with the policies of the Nazi Party.

Chapter 18

Telegrams and Reports

The Höfle Telegram

In the year 2000 an important document was discovered at the Public Record Office in London. It was a one-page document dated 11 January 1943 which contained the notes from 'cables'. It was marked 'Top Secret' and was sent by Herman Höfle to Adolf Eichmann in Berlin. Another identical one was sent to SS Obersturmbannführer Franz Heim in Krakow, in German-occupied Poland.

The coded telegram informed the recipients how many Jews had been murdered in the different extermination camps in 1942. The telegram included four letters: (B), (S), (T) and (L) – Belzec, Sobibor, Treblinka and Lublin-Majdanek. The numbers against each letter were the numbers of Jews who had been murdered at each camp. When compared with the numbers of arrivals as recorded on the Holocaust train records, they didn't always add up, showing more people having been murdered than had arrived at the camps.

The Holocaust trains were run by *Deutsche Reichsbahn* (German Railways) and the SS paid them the price of a third-class ticket for each person who was transported from the ghettos to the extermination camps. Children under 4 went free. The German Transport Authority collected the monies from the SS on behalf of the *Reichsbahn*. The SS were charged per boxcar and not by the number of people who were actually on the train. Each transport would contain fifty boxcars, with an allowance of fifty people per boxcar. This would give a figure of 2,500 people per transport, but the boxcars would often contain twice that number, or more; it wasn't uncommon for the transports to have as many as 7,000 people on board. So thousands more people

```
                                                    GPDD 355a    2.

  12. OMX de OMQ              1000           89 ? ?
      Geheime Reichssache! An das Reichssicherheitshauptamt, zu
      Händen SS Obersturmbannführer EICHMANN, BERLIN ...rest missed..

13/15. OLQ de OMQ             1005           83 234 250
      Geheime Reichssache! An den Befehlshaber der Sicherheitspol.,
      zu Händen SS Obersturmbannführer HEIM, KRAKAU.
      Betr: 14-tägige Meldung Einsatz REINHART. Bezug: dort.
      Fs. Zugang bis 31.12.42, L 12761,B 0, S 515, T 10335 zusammen
      23611. Stand... 31.12.42, L 24733, B 434508, S 101370,
      T 71355, zusammen 1274166.
      SS und Pol.führer LUBLIN, HOEFLE, Sturmbannführer.
```

The Höfle Telegram.

actually arrived at the death camps than what the train transport records showed.

The telegram was intercepted and decoded at Bletchley Park, but they appear not to have realised the significance of what they were reading. It stated that for the year ending 1942 a total of 1,274,146 Jews were murdered at the extermination camps.

The Riegner Telegram

This was dated 8 August 1942 and sent by Gerhart Riegner, the then Secretary of the World Jewish Congress in Geneva, to its offices in London and New York.

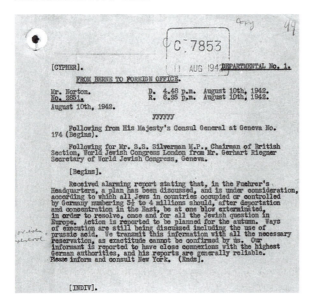

The Riegner Telegram.

The telegram contained alarming information about Nazi Germany's intention to murder all European Jews. Riegner had be informed of the plans by German industrialist Eduard Schulte. It was read with disbelief in England and the United States.

The Jäger Report

This was written by Karl Jäger, commander of Einsatzkommando 3, one of the sections of Einsatzgruppe A attached to Army Group North during the invasion of the Soviet Union which began on 22 June 1941.

```
                                   Blatt 6.

                                   -Übertrag:
                                                                    99 804

12.9.41  Wilna-Stadt   993 Juden,1670 Jüdinn.771 J.-Kind.    3 334
17.9.41    "      "    337  "      687  "      247  "         1 271
                       und 4 lit.Kommunisten
20.9.41  Nemencing     128 Juden, 176 Jüdinn. 99    "            403
22.9.41  Novo-Wilejka  468  "  ,  495  "      196    "        1 159
24.9.41  Riese         512  "      744  "      511   "        1 767
25.9.41  Jahiunai      215  "      229  "      131   "          575
27.9.41  Eysisky       989  "     1636  "      821   "        3 446
30.9.41  Trakai        366  "      483  "      597   "        1 446
4.10.41  Wilna-Stadt   432  "     1115  "      436   "        1 983
6.10.41  Semiliski     213  "      359  "      390   "          962
9.10.41  Svenciany    1169  "     1840  "      717   "        3 726
16.10.41 Wilna-Stadt   382  "      507  "      257   "        1 146
21.10.41   "      "    718  "     1063  "      586   "        2 367
25.10.41   "      "     -   "     1766  "      812   "        2 578
27.10.41   "      "    946  "      184  "       73   "        1 203
30.10.41   "      "    382  "      789  "      362   "        1 533
6.11.41    "      "    340  "      749  "      252   "        1 341
19.11.41   "      "     76  "       77  "       18   "          171
19.11.41   "      "         6 Kriegsgefangene, 8 Polen           14
20.11.41   "      "     3          "                              3
25.11.41   "      "         9 Juden, 46 Jüdinnen, 8 J.-Kinder,   64
                           1 Pole wegen Waffenbesitz u.Besitz
                           von anderem Kriegsgerät.

Teilkommando des EK.3
       in Minsk
vom 28.9.-17.10.41:

              Pleschnitze,
              Bicholin,
              Scak,
              Bober,
              Uzda

                       620 Juden,1285 Jüdinnen,1126 J.-Kind.   3 050
                       und 19 Kommunisten

                                                             133 346

    Vor Übernahme der sicherheitspol.Aufgaben durch das EK.3,  4 000
Juden durch Progrome und Exekutionen - ausschliesslich von
Partisanen - liquidiert.

                                                      u.     137 346
```

The Jäger Report provided details of the daily murders carried out by a single Einsatzkommando.

It was a detailed report of the number of daily murders that had been carried out in Lithuania, Latvia, and Belarus by just one Einsatzkommando between June and November 1941, although the bottom photograph on the previous page only contains the details of the last three months covered by the nine-page report. The report was discovered by the Soviet Army when they recaptured Lithuania from the Germans, but it wasn't known about in the West until 1963, during the trial of Hans Globke.

The Korherr Report

This was a sixteen-page report on how the Holocaust was proceeding throughout German-occupied Europe. It was dated January 1943 and sent to Himmler by Doctor Richard Korherr, Chief Inspector of the Statistical Bureau of the SS. The photograph opposite shows page 9 of the report.

It started by estimating that the number of European Jews had fallen by some four million between 1937 and 31 December 1942, including those who had emigrated, and that between October 1939 and 31 December 1942, 1,274,000 Jews had been murdered in the death camps of Poland.

The report included the following from Korherr:

It must not be overlooked in this respect that of the deaths of Soviet Russian Jews in the occupied Eastern territories only a part was recorded, whereas deaths in the rest of European Russia and at the front are not included at all. In addition there are movements of Jews inside Russia to the Asian part which are unknown to us. The movement of Jews from the European countries outside the German influence is also of a largely unknown order of magnitude. On the whole European Jewry should since 1933, i.e. in the first decade of National Socialist Germany, have lost half of its population.

After the war Korherr had a somewhat different story to tell when he sent a letter to *Der Spiegel*. He said he had no knowledge of the Holocaust at the time and that he only found out about it after it

-9-   . *AC · 51 ?4*

V. DIE EVAKUIERUNG DER JUDEN

Die Evakuierung der Juden löste, wenigstens im Reichsgebiet,
die Auswanderung der Juden ab. Sie wurde seit dem Verbot der
jüdischen Auswanderung ab Herbst 1941 in großem Stile vor-
bereitet und im Jahre 1942 im gesamten Reichsgebiet weit-
gehend durchgeführt. In der Bilanz des Judentums erscheint
sie als "Abwanderung".
Bis 1.1.1943 wanderten nach den Zusammenstellungen des
Reichssicherheitshauptamtes ab:

aus dem Altreich mit Sudetenland	100 516	Juden
aus der Ostmark	47 555	"
aus dem Protektorat	69 677	"
Zusammen	217 748	Juden

In diesen Zahlen sind auch die ins Altersghetto Theresienstadt evakuierten Juden enthalten.

Die gesamten Evakuierungen ergaben im Reichsgebiet einschl.
Ostgebieten und darüber hinaus im deutschen Macht- und Ein-
flußbereich in Europa von Oktober 1939 oder später bis zum
31.12.1942 folgende Zahlen:

1. Evakuierung von Juden aus Baden
   und der Pfalz nach Frankreich.......   6 504 Juden
2. Evakuierung von Juden aus dem Reichsgebiet einschl. Protektorat und
   Bezirk Bialystok nach Osten......... 170 642   "
3. Evakuierung von Juden aus dem Reichsgebiet und dem Protektorat
   nach Theresienstadt.................   87 193   "
4. Transportierung von Juden aus den
   Ostprovinzen nach dem russischen
   Osten: ....1 449 692   "

   Es wurden durchgeschleust
   durch die Lager im General-
   gouvernement...................... 1 274 166 Juden
   durch die Lager im Warthegau.....   145 301   "
5. Evakuierung von Juden aus anderen
   Ländern, nämlich:

   Frankreich (soweit vor dem
   10.11.1942 besetzt).............. 41 911 Juden
   Niederlande..................... 38 571   "
   Belgien......................... 16 886   "
   Norwegen........................   532

The Korherr report.

came to light at the end of the war. He also denied that his report of January 1943 had been written on the orders of Himmler, and further wrote:

> *The statement that I had mentioned that over a million Jews had died in the camps of the Generalregierung and the Warthegau through special treatment is also inaccurate. I must protest against the word 'died' in this context. It was the very word 'Sonderbehandlung' that led me to call the RSHA by phone and ask what this word meant. I was given the answer that these were the Jews who were settled in the Lublin district.*

The Gerstein Report

This was written by Obersturmführer Kurt Gerstein of the Waffen-SS. Head of Technical Disinfection Services, it was he who supplied Rudolf Höss at Auschwitz with the Zyklon B used in the gas chambers, and conducted negotiations with the owners of the company who manufactured it. On 22 April 1945 he surrendered in the Allied-occupied town of Reutlingen and was sent to nearby Rottweil where he was placed in 'honourable captivity' in the Hotel Mohren. There he wrote his report.

He wrote that on 18 August 1942 he visited the Belzec extermination camp, where he witnessed the arrival of a transport which contained 45 wagons and 6,700 people. When the doors of the transport wagons were opened, it was found that 1,450 of were dead. He then wrote about the selection and gassing of those who were to die.

The final part of Gerstein's report describes his attempts to circulate what he had seen at Belzec to the outside world. He met the secretary of the Swedish legation in Berlin and told him what he had witnessed. In vain he requested that he inform his government and those of the other Allies, pointing out that the longer he delayed, the more lives would be lost. He even tried to have the information passed on to the Pope via the ecclesiastical diplomat in Berlin, Cesare Orsenigo, but the Pope's representative refused to meet him.

Gerstein was taking a great risk, because if word had reached senior Nazis or the Gestapo, he would have undoubtedly been arrested and executed.

The Cornides Report

Wilhelm Cornides was a sergeant in the German Army during the occupation of Poland. On 30 August 1942, on a train to Chelm, he wrote a personal journal containing views and comments about which he dared not speak to anybody else.

En route he spoke to a policemen and railway workers about the very long freight trains that they passed on their journey: it was then that he found out for the first time about the Holocaust. The policeman knew all about what the Nazis were doing to the Jews. The journal did not come to light until 1959.

In December 1946 Cornides founded the *Europa-Archiv*, the journal of the German Council on Foreign Relations, which is still in existence today.

Einsatzgruppen Operational Situation Reports

For the period June to April 1941 these document the progress of the Einsatzgruppen in Operation Barbarossa. The reports were sent to Berlin to the Chief of the Secret Police.

In Closing

How did so many supposedly intelligent German people suddenly became deranged killers, sadistic brutalisers of innocent people, and individuals who could kill in cold blood without question, bereft of any empathy for their victims?

The Holocaust wasn't a war, in which there is at least some justification for killing; it was the systematic murder of millions of innocent people for no other reason than that they were Jews, a group of people unfortunate enough to be disliked by Adolf Hitler. For the Nazis, it was not sufficient to steal the Jews' belongings, property, jewellery and money; it wasn't sufficient to deport them to other countries: they wanted to kill them, murder every one of them, men, women and children.

Those who perpetrated these crimes were, before the war, mostly normal individuals with normal feelings, yet as soon as anti-Jewish fever took hold, they changed into deranged, delusional psychopaths.

For the Jews, there were no rules to protect them anymore. People could say or do whatever they liked against them, and there were no punishments. What would happen if you woke up tomorrow morning to hear that there was suddenly no law? That everyone could do whatever they wanted, without limit. Well, that's exactly what happened in Nazi Germany in relation to the Jews. It cannot and must not ever happen again.

Sources

britishnewspaperarchive.co.uk
bergenbelsen.co.uk
spartacus-educational.com
jewishgen.org
thoughtco.com
sobiborinterview.nl
holocaustresearchroject.org
Belzec, Rudolf Reder (1946)

Index